UNCOMPLETED MISSION

Pages 124,
125-26 v. important.
128-9
NOTE African quest for Relig identity
within the RC.

Pages 132 - 142
145 - 156

UNCOMPLETED MISSION

Christianity and Exclusivism

Kwesi A. Dickson

ORBIS BOOKS

Maryknoll, New York 10545

The Catholic Foreign Mission Society of America (Maryknoll) recruits and trains people for overseas missionary service. Through Orbis Books, Maryknoll aims to foster the international dialogue that is essential to mission. The books published, however, reflect the opinions of their authors and are not meant to represent the official position of the society.

Library of Congress Cataloging-in-Publication Data

Dickson, Kwesi A.
 Uncompleted mission: Christianity and exclusivism / Kwesi A. Dickson.
  p. cm.
 Includes bibliographical references and index.
 ISBN 0-88344-751-7
 1. Missions. 2. Christianity and culture. 3. Religious tolerance—Christianity. 4. Christianity and other religions.
 I. Title.
 BV2063.D48 1991
 261—dc20   91-11351
                                                     CIP

To my wife
Cecilia

Contents

Preface ix

Introduction 1

1. **Jewish Attitudes toward Other Peoples up till the Time of Christ** 7
   Israel among the Nations 9
   The Return from Exile 13
   Continuity between Israelite and Other Religions 15
   Malachi and Israel's Relation with the World 21
   Non-Jews and the Covenant 25

2. **The Early Church: Questions and Attitudes** 29
   The Gospels: Jewish Tradition and Attitudes toward Gentiles 30
   Mission in The Acts of the Apostles 34
   Stephen's Views on Jewish Traditions 37
   The Role of Antioch 40
   Paul's Speeches at Lystra and Athens 42
   The Council of Jerusalem 43
   Galatians and Mission to the Gentiles 48
   Paul's Attitude toward Circumcision 52
   Attitudes toward Pagan Practices 54
   Conclusion: The Acts, Galatians, and Mission 57

3. **Biblical and Other Influences upon Mission** 60
   The Old Testament and Mission 61
   The New Testament and Mission 67

The Reformation's Effect on Modern Missions   76
The Influences of Modern European Scholars   82
Dominance of Exclusivism   85
Creeds and Their Significance   86

4. Strategy Pronouncements and Their Significance   **92**
Adaptation   93
Importance of Respect for All Religions   97
Vatican II and Official Catholic Policy   100
Suggestions for Improving Church Policy   106
*Dynamic Interaction between Christian and Other
     Faiths   110*
*Three Approaches To Discovering a Distinctive
     Christianity   116*
Salvation Religions   119

5. Exclusivism and the Church Today   **124**
Movements in the African Quest for Religious Identity   126
The Independent Churches   129
Biblical Interpretation   132
African Life, Religion, and Culture   142
An African Approach to the Scriptures   145

6. Conclusion   **157**

Notes   **163**

Bibliography   **173**

Index   **175**

Preface

There are two facts about the church which have held a fascination for me over the years. Since its inception, the church has proclaimed Christ as savior, inviting people to change their allegiance and follow Christ. The Acts of the Apostles notes with evident satisfaction the increase in church membership which attended the apostles' preaching. There is a second fact, and that is, the church itself tends to resist change — it expects those who hear the message and accept it to conform to what the church recognizably is. Of course, given the church's conviction that it is the body of Christ, the church believes itself to have the responsibility to nurture its converts so that they remain members of that body; hence Luke's note that the early converts "devoted themselves to the apostles' teaching." However, what does not seem to have sufficiently engaged the attention of the church is the possibility of a convert's humanity being distorted in the attempt to achieve conformity with the institutional specification with respect to the style of church membership, interpreting the Bible, proclaiming the gospel message, and so forth.

When I received an invitation to give four lectures to a Winter School organized at Mansfield College, Oxford, by American friends of the college, in the first week of January 1987, I welcomed the opportunity not only to visit my old college, but also to give some thought to these two facts about the church and their implications. This study is the outcome, made up of a reworked version of the lectures (the present five grew out of the original four) which I gave on that occasion.

This does not pretend to be an exhaustive study. It follows a particular line of inquiry, raising among others the issue of what the church, given the strengths, and especially the weaknesses, of its mode of operation, might be owing to its Scriptures and its history. Of course, Africa was never far from my thoughts as I pondered this issue, but I dare say that this study will have relevance for the church, historic and independent, wherever it may be found.

It was while in the process of finalizing the manuscript that the Methodist church, Ghana, at its Annual Conference in August 1988, made me its President-Designate. This created in me an even greater consciousness of the urgency of this study's theme, the challenge posed by it seeming even less avoidable than ever.

I must express my gratitude to my wife, without whose patient retrieval of notes scattered everywhere this study would have taken much longer to complete.

GHANA
1991

Introduction

As long as the church remains in the world, mission will be its raison d'être, for the church has its origin in God's mission in Christ. When it came into being the Christian church owed something to the concern of the Jews to bring within the walls of Judaism those non-Jews who were attracted to it; especially, however, did the church owe its life to what was understood to be a command by Christ to go out and make disciples everywhere. The story of the mission of the church since is most impressive, a story of determination and commitment, of love and concern, of sacrifice and death.

Despite the centuries of achievement, however, no one seriously believes that the church's missionary task has become any simpler today; on the contrary, it has become an even more awesome undertaking. For one thing, the mission field remains practically as wide as ever. "There are two billion people—and their number is increasing day by day—who have never, or barely, heard the Gospel message."[1] To this must be added the fact that many who were once in the church as members, and even as ordained officiants, have left the church, or keep their ties with it to the barest minimum. This, needless to say, poses a great challenge to the church, which challenge it is endeavoring to meet by a variety of imaginative means: through church-inspired urban renewal programs; industrial missions; programs of innovative theological study which firmly situate those undergoing training within the context of their communities in order to make them into more creative and effective links between society and the church (as against residential training which can have important negative effects on the trainees in the matter of how the church is perceived in relation to the world); and, generally, through theological renewal which endeavors to make theology less the esoteric discipline it has tended to be over the centuries, and more like the mirror into which the believer might look and see in action Christ's message for the viewer, as well as for society at large.

The reference just made to theology brings us to an element in mission which tends to be neglected — at least, it does not seem to be viewed with a commensurate sense of urgency. That element is the reorientation of the message in order to lead to maturer faith those who are within the church, both those who are committed to the church's teaching as it is, and those who seem to be committed to the church as a body whose worship and other activities punctuate life with such moments of relief as engender a sense of general well-being, but nothing else.

It is not as if the church is unaware of the kinds of people, within and without, who must be reached in obedience to Christ's command; in many different ways the church, particularly in the West where interest in it seems to have waned considerably over the years, has been endeavoring to meet the growing challenge, as already indicated. However, while on the one hand the church considers itself led by the example of Christ, on the other hand certain elements in the church's life and work, which have over the years become part of the church's very identity in society, tend to limit its effectiveness as an agent of God's mission. Indeed, the church seems to exercise as much care in its endeavor to reach members of society as it does in distancing itself from them. Thus in Western countries requirements for theological education are such that fewer and fewer interested persons can qualify for such training. In a number of instances theological education involves theological students taking university courses which may not have in view the church and its concerns, the church having had nothing to do with designing those courses. Some would say this is just as well, if the church does not seem to have the right vision and goals, but then the university as such may not have the kind of concerns which should define what the church should be about. A similar situation is developing with alarming rapidity in Africa, where theological education is fast becoming the preserve of the few who have the right qualifications, especially considering that such education is usually carried out through the medium of the colonial language. Furthermore, in African countries few Christians seem to be aware of the serious theological questions being raised by the worsening socioeconomic and political situation, and its impact on their societies in the form of lowered moral standards. The worse the situation gets, the more people, Christians included, become preoccupied with the struggle for survival—*personal* survival. A situation of this sort raises questions of significant theological import, and these must have an impact on the church's mission.

It is in the area of culture that the church, through its movement from continent to continent, country to country, and people to people, has seemed particularly exclusivist. Undoubtedly this attitude played a significant role in shaping the methods and goals of mission and thus the life of the fledgling churches in the mission areas, especially in Africa. Exclusivist thinking starts from the basis of one's own perspective—and ends there. The possibility of matters being viewed also from the bona fide perspective of the other person or group does not readily come into play. Exclusivism has manifested itself in a variety of ways: in keeping at a distance the local cultural reality, either because no serious thought is given to the possibility of the development of a form of Christianity which is not necessarily identical with the missionary's brand of it, or because the local culture is seen as a force which nullifies the missionary's dedicated efforts. It has manifested itself in the operation of church administration systems which are modeled on patterns developed in the European context, and in the training of clergy which often leaves the finished products powerless in the face of life around them and thus unsuited to minister within their own cultural area. It must be made clear that these comments pertain not only to the missionary attitudes which brought the church into being in Africa, but also to the generally unimaginative outlook of the African church, which is now largely independent but is still inclined to adhere closely to the systems of belief and practice inherited from churches elsewhere. Thus the exclusivism which emanates from the missionary endeavors has come to characterize the former mission churches, to the extent that even the conviction that the faith necessarily touches the totality of one's circumstances has sometimes been expressed using categories of thought taken from theological systems developed elsewhere. In other words, theological ideas from elsewhere have simply been adapted to local conditions, with predictable consequences: there has been no real engagement between Christianity and African life and thought. Even if a certain level of relevance has been achieved, this has been offset by the fact that what is essentially an exclusivist attitude is inherent in adaptionism.

Now the Christian faith does lay claim to a message which has to do with the unrepeatable act of God coming in God's son Jesus Christ who, on the cross, took on the sins of men and women of every age and place, and triumphed. In the sense of its being unrepeatable, it is an exclusive message. The spirit of truth promised by Christ ever enlightens humanity, enabling people of every age and place to understand what God has done in Christ. The issue is how the implications of this exclusiveness are to be understood. In the history of the church, claims have been made which have set the church apart from the world, thus making the church's apparent interest in men and women as children of God seem at best unreal, and at worst downright hypocritical. Thus it was popular at one time to claim such distinctiveness for Christianity so as to imply that all other religions were totally false. No serious religious thinker today takes this view to be a reasonable option. There is also the claim which characterized much missionary activity throughout the centuries down to the modern era, that the faith and its expression constitute a fixed and unalterable reality—they have to be appropriated in precisely that form. Thus the exclusiveness of the gospel message comes to be defined not so much by the fact of God in Christ reaching towards humanity as by the presenter's apprehension of that fact.

This has been a source of much questioning and confusion. Thus in the modern missionary period every attempt was made to ensure that the mission church was as much as possible a copy of the church out of which the missionary had come. Earlier, in the days of the apostles, Jewish Christians, some of whom embarked on a mission probably before law-free preaching was heard from the likes of Paul, insisted on Gentile converts observing what were essentially Jewish religious restrictions which in Jewish tradition had been placed upon proselytes.

Since the completion of the canon of Scriptures the church has been guided by a body of traditions, one aspect of which seems to regard exclusivist attitudes as a realistic option. As the opening chapter of this study shows, a strong exclusivist strain runs through the Old Testament, and this would appear to have been picked up in New Testament times, as demonstrated in the second chapter. The rest of this study traces this exclusivist strain through the Reformers to our day, and draws attention to a fact of importance: the Bible, which is part of the church's tradition, needs to be carefully studied and expounded, for surely exclusivist tendencies contradict the very concept of mission which is the church's raison d'être. Any approach to the Bible that fails to recognize exclusivism for what it is cannot but detract from the true significance of two central biblical concepts.

There is, first, the biblical affirmation that the world was created by God, and human beings created in God's own image. This affirmation runs right through the Scriptures, and is epitomized, among other things, by Christ's concern for all kinds of people, both Jews and non-Jews. Properly understood, therefore, the missionary's task is to bring the gospel message to God's own people. It is interesting in this connection to consider the New Testament language of the new creation and its possible effect on the church's thinking, particularly with respect to fulfilling its missionary task. Paul writes, "Therefore, if any one is in Christ, there is a new creation; the old has passed away, behold, the new has come" (2 Cor. 5:17). And "neither circumcision accounts for anything, nor uncircumcision, but a new creation" (Gal. 6:15). On the basis of verses such as these the church, consisting of those who affirm the lordship of Christ, may speak of itself as part of the new creation. By that very fact, those who are not in the church belong to the old creation which has ceased to be. Evidently language of this kind, legitimate and meaningful as it might be in its New Testament context, can inveigle one into a triumphalist attitude vis-à-vis those to whom the gospel message is being preached, especially where, as happened in the era of modern missions, the missionaries came from the land of the colonial rulers. Properly understood, the doctrine of creation enjoins Christians to recognize that differences among the peoples of the world are in accordance with God's wisdom. To suppose that some traditions might be more authentic than others is to ignore the fact that different cultural traditions are relative, because each defines a people as it is, created in the image of God.

The other biblical affirmation of central value for evaluating the exclusivist attitude is the incarnation. That Christ came and shared our humanity is clearly evidenced in the pages of the gospels. Excessive pietistic zeal might have led to a Docetist view of Christ as one who only appeared to be human, but the gospel writers, without exception, picture Jesus as one whose humanity was there for all to see. He might have criticized aspects of his people's religio-cultural tradition, but he did not disown it; he taught about "the end," but he brought comfort to the sick and the poor and the outcasts; he castigated Jerusalem, and wept over her obduracy. In these and various other ways the incarnation is presented as an exemplification of God's love for every aspect of God's creation. Exclusivism can be a denial of the richness of this coming.

To return to the comment about the once-for-allness of the gospel message, this exclusiveness lies, properly understood, in the fact that the God who created humanity made a supreme sacrifice to give God's son for the good of a humanity which had chosen not to recognize its creator. Thus the essential characteristic of this exclusiveness is, paradoxically, that God seeks community with the human race—with all peoples. Exclusivism misses something of this paradox.

1

Jewish Attitudes toward Other Peoples up till the Time of Christ

---

An examination of the Old Testament is a necessary preliminary to the study of mission in the New Testament. After all, it constituted the Scriptures of the early church which, when it emerged, owed much to its Judaistic parentage. What the Old Testament says about other peoples and their traditions, then, must be presumed to have exercised some influence on the early church as it sought to relate to non-Jewish peoples.

The Old Testament does contain indications of the attitudes which the Jews adopted toward non-Jews and their religious traditions up till the emergence of the Christian church. To say this is not to suggest that it offers clear-cut material on the subject, for it is not a textbook of ancient religion. Not only does the Old Testament not have a word for religion, neither does it set out to discuss religion in any theoretical way. To go to the Old Testament for material which deals specifically with the nature of religion is to return nearly empty-handed.

Nevertheless, the Old Testament does contain information which enables us to see how ancient Israel viewed her religion in relation to others' religions. There are two main avenues by which Israel's attitudes are conveyed: the conviction that Yahweh is Israel's God, and the record of her relations with other peoples as Israel tested and tried her nationhood. These two avenues are closely linked, however, for in the final analysis the Old Testament is about God. God's dealings with Israel reveal God's ways and underline the agonies experienced by Israel as she battled time and again to maintain her nationhood under God. Thus Israel's attitudes are revealed in her interaction with non-Jews. In view of the number of peoples which feature in Israel's tortuous story, references to other religious traditions are not lacking, though they are not presented as reasoned statements. They are simply the reactions of a people who, born in slavery, believed itself to have been saved by Yahweh, and spent its adulthood going through the hard school of national survival.

There is a strong Old Testament tradition that Israel stood in a special relationship with God, a relationship epitomized by the images of choice (Deut. 7:7) and covenant (Deut. 5:2). Israel was God's own people, chosen by God and brought into a covenant relationship with God, which made Israel into a "people." That the choice and covenant concepts were interpreted by some in Israel to mean that Israel specially deserved this divine attention is clear from the attacks made upon this kind of thinking in several passages which insist that God chose Israel without her having deserved this attention (Deut. 9:4–5). The deuteronomic movement, in particular, made much of the covenant idea, with the result that the biblical account of the life and thought of Israel has been so written as to reflect the view that there was a special bond between Yahweh and Israel. On no account were the people of Israel to forget that they owed allegiance to Yahweh who would not share Israel with a rival. In this connection it has been observed:

> There are three features regarding this covenant theology which stand out very strikingly, and which lend to it a theological character of a unique kind. These concern its relationship to Israel as a nation, to the land of Canaan as God's gift, and to a written collection of laws and instructions described as *torah*. All three features have been passed on from this Deuteronomic nucleus to the Old Tes-

tament as a whole, thereby making it a "covenant literature"—an Old Testament.[1]

Indeed, the Deuteronomist refers to the Israelites as children
of Yahweh (Deut. 14:1). While it may not be necessary to pos-
tulate, on the basis of this, a cult in which early Israel invoked
Yahweh as father, nevertheless the expression strongly implies
a special bond between Yahweh and the Israelites who are
described as "a people holy to the Lord" (Deut. 14:2). To say
that this conviction is reflected in Israel's history, which was one
of constant interaction with other peoples, from the Egyptians
to the Romans, is to make an understatement, for indeed a
wealth of references cites her distinctiveness as a people which
considered itself to be in a relationship with Yahweh.

ISRAEL AMONG THE NATIONS

The period of the sojourn in Egypt is a potentially exciting
one, from the point of view of the light it might throw upon the
development of Israel's religion; unfortunately much less is
known about it than one would like. In the century before the
Hebrews were allowed to leave Egypt on their protracted journey to Canaan, the Egyptian king Amenophis IV (1372-1354
B.C.E.) initiated an interesting religious experiment: he issued a
proclamation that all the Egyptian gods were nonexistent, with
the exception of Aton (or Aten), the Sun Disc.[2] Amenophis IV
took steps to popularize this monotheism, firmly suppressing the
other gods. The fascinating suggestion has been made that he
pushed this reform through because the then state cult of Amon
was too exclusively Egyptian to attract the many Asiatic groups
which had migrated to Egypt. A god with a more popular appeal
was needed. However that may be, we do not know what the
Hebrews living in Egypt at the time thought of this religious
reform. It turned out to be a short-lived reform, however, for
with the death of its originator the process was reversed, and
the gods came back into prominence. In the very next century,
perhaps around a hundred years following the death of Amenophis IV, the Hebrews left Egypt on the great trek to Canaan.
The suggestion that there is a connection between the Egyp-

tian monotheism under Amenophis IV and Mosaic religion may
not be too readily dismissed even though it is not easy to sub-
stantiate it satisfactorily. Ringgren has in fact observed that no
such connection could be claimed since the Yahweh proclaimed
by Moses was not a sun god.[3] All the same, it may with some
justification be argued, on the basis of the nature of the Mosaic
faith, that the Israelites reacted negatively to the polytheism that
prevailed before and after Amenophis IV, the Decalogue being
suggestive in this regard. In its opening injunction the making
of gods is prohibited (Exod. 20:3, 4; Deut. 5:7, 8) in the kind of
language which seems to be reminiscent of Egyptian religious
practices. The prohibition of any "likeness of anything that is in
heaven above" could very well have been a reaction to the Egyptian practice of worshiping the sun,[4] moon and stars. With
respect to the commandment which forbids the making of "any
likeness of anything . . . that is in the earth beneath, or that is
in the water under the earth," it might be observed that the
Egyptians gave human and animal forms to the gods which they
worshiped. The crocodile, for example, a creature that lived in
the water "under the earth," was one such form. Noth thus puts
the purpose of this prohibition: "Israel is forbidden any image
so that the people cannot even make the attempt to gain power
over God or that which is of God."[5] Any religious activity that
would negate the belief that Yahweh was incomparable was
unacceptable.

The deuteronomic reconstruction of the history of the Israelite settlement in Canaan is to a certain extent a theological
statement which sees the people of God as not living together
with the pagan peoples, the latter having been quickly dispos-
sessed and decimated. Of course, to consider the account of the
conquest in Joshua 1–12 as simply theological is not to do full
justice to it. Indeed archeological research has shown that several Canaanite cities were violently destroyed, usually by fire, in
the thirteenth century B.C.E., the very century in which the Israelites entered Canaan, which thus accords with the description
of a violent confrontation, as found in the Book of Joshua,
between the Israelites and the Canaanites. Nevertheless, the
distinctive style adopted in the Joshua account arises out of the
conviction that since the land of Canaan had been promised to

the Israelites, surely its possession by them could not be thwarted by those who did not know Yahweh!

It is in keeping with this that the Israelites were forbidden to adopt pagan life and thought (Deut. 8:19-20, 18:9-14, etc.). For example, they were not to indulge in those mourning rites which were commonly practiced in the ancient Near East (Deut. 14:1; Isa. 15:2, 22:12; Jer. 16:6, 41:5; Ezek. 7:18, etc.). One such rite was to deliberately gash oneself (Deut. 14:1) as a demonstration of one's feelings; another was to make "baldness on your foreheads," a reference to the custom whereby the hair of the one in grief was shaved off and buried with the dead as an offering to the dead (cf. Lev. 21:5). Deuteronomy 14:3-21 warns the Israelites against eating "any abominable thing" (cf. Dan. 1:8) and maintains a distinction between clean and unclean creatures. The grounds upon which this distinction is drawn are not explained, but the swine, it is known, was a sacred animal at Ugarit, while those birds which were not to be eaten were largely predatory birds which would prey on other creatures which might not be considered clean.[6] These laws were meant to underline the distinctiveness of Israel, and it is in this context that Israel's abhorence of Canaanite religion, with its sensuousness, must be seen. Indeed, certain episodes in Genesis seem to contain echoes of Israel's convictions regarding the destructive nature of Canaanite culture. Thus the first attempt to till the land and plant a vineyard, which was a normal feature of Canaanite agriculture, resulted in drunkenness (Gen. 9:18-27), while the story of the Tower of Babel seems to be decrying that cultural pride which had produced the famous ziggurat of Babylon (Gen. 11:1-9).

Furthermore, the tradition of Israel's distinctiveness explains such practices as *herem*. Reference has already been made to the deuteronomic account of the Israelite conquest and the violent elimination of the inhabitants who worshiped strange gods, so that "they may not teach you to do according to all their abominable practices, which they have done in the service of their gods, and so to sin against the Lord your God (Deut. 20:18; also 7:1-5). To underline the importance of obedience to Yahweh Deuteronomy makes it clear that the Israelites will have only themselves to blame if they go after other gods: "Like the nations that the Lord makes to perish before you, so shall you perish, because you would not obey the voice of the Lord your God" (Deut. 8:20).

As to the heathens' gods, these were at first treated as real enough; indeed, the Decalogue presupposes the existence of other gods, though Israel is forbidden to give them allegiance since this would be a flagrant breach of the covenant relationship with God. However, that dedicated Yahwists considered the gods to be powerless is clear, for example, in Elijah's challenge to the Baal prophets during the Mount Carmel episode. The sarcasm in Elijah's words addressed to the Baal prophets is unmistakable: "Cry aloud, for he is a god; either he is musing, or he has gone aside, or he is on a journey, or perhaps he is asleep and must be awakened" (1 Kings 18:27). Later writings refuse to accord the nations' gods any reality whatsoever: "I am the first and I am the last; besides me there is no god" (Isa. 44:6).

Despite these convictions, Israel's conflicts with hostile powers throughout the period of the kings took their toll on her religion. It was the accepted practice in the ancient world that the vassal status necessitated the adoption of the victor's cults. The biblical account does not spare Manasseh for adopting foreign cults as extensively as he did (2 Kings 21); his religious policies form the background to the reforms carried out by King Josiah in the seventh century B.C.E. The account of those reforms refers more than once to the fact of Judah's kings having adopted un-Israelite religious practices (2 Kings 23:1ff.). Such adoption was more likely to occur during the Assyrian period of Judah, that is, following 701 B.C.E., though, of course, it had been known before then. While in Damascus to pay homage to the Assyrian king Tiglath-Pileser III, King Ahaz of Judah (734-715 B.C.E.) obtained a blueprint for an Assyrian altar and saw to its construction in the Jerusalem temple. Thus the reforms of King Josiah, as well as those of King Hezekiah about one hundred years earlier (2 Kings 18:1ff.), had a politico-religious significance—they expressed Judah's political independence, which would free her from having to encourage religious practices which would make the people of Judah traitors of Yahwism. Of course, the reforms were not an unqualified success.

Hezekiah's reforms gave way to Manasseh's recognition of the Assyrian overlordship and the resultant adoption of un-Israelite practices, while we see from Ezekial's prophecies that, Josiah's strict religious measures notwithstanding, the Jerusalem temple continued to harbor strange religious objects and practices (Ezek. 8), to the utter distaste of the prophet.

In view of all this the exiles of 721 B.C.E. and 586 B.C.E. must have been uncomfortable experiences, because they seemed to imply the futility of depending upon Yahweh, the national God. The account of the events following the 721 B.C.E. episode contains a reference of some interest. The vicissitudes of those whom the Assyrians brought to Palestine from parts of their empire served to underline the conviction that to live in safety in the land of Israel it was essential to follow "the law of the god of the land" (2 Kings 17:27); no other law would do. The compilers of the biblical account have so placed this episode — in a context of lax religious lifestyle (2 Kings 17:24-41) — as to underline their concern: the importance of obedience to Yahweh. As far as the exile of 586 B.C.E. is concerned, if the exiles had uncomfortable experiences, these did not arise from their being tortured or generally maltreated. On the contrary, the exiles enjoyed considerable freedom in Babylon: of association, of economic improvement, and of communication with the homeland. The really difficult adjustment they had to make was in the area of worship — how to "sing the Lord's song in a foreign land" (Ps. 137:4), something they were having difficulty doing. Quite possibly some of the exiles lost their faith since their status as exiles seemed to be indicative of Yahweh's impotence — could this be the God who had led their ancestors out of Egypt? Others — and these would seem to have exerted some influence — were led by the experience to the conviction that their national survival was closely linked to the survival of their faith; hence the strict observance of circumcision and the sabbath, and the rewriting of the existing records of their history to reflect the deuteronomic teaching that obedience to God led to peace and prosperity, while disobedience brought punishment in its wake.

THE RETURN FROM EXILE

The sixth-century disagreement between the returned exiles and the Samaritans in connection with the rebuilding of the temple is a significant element in the Jews' attempt to protect Yahwism against what were considered as deleterious influences. The Samaritans had informed the Jews that they were as much worshipers of Yahweh as the latter (Ezra 4:1f.). There is no question but that the Jewish reaction to the Samaritans' request was far from reasonable—the consequent Samaritan attitude to the Jews and their traditions was not reasonable, either. For the Jews to suppose that the people of the former northern kingdom had all intermarried with those whom the Assyrians brought in from the far reaches of the empire, or were all descended from such intermarriage, was to show a certain prejudice. Not all the northerners had been taken into exile, and it most reasonably has to be assumed that there were northerners who had kept their identity intact, so that the Samaritan claim to be worshipers of Yahweh deserved serious consideration. The Jews simply could not ignore the fact that the northern remnant had been sharing its land with nonworshipers of Yahweh.

In the fifth and fourth centuries the desire to establish Judaism on a sound footing led Nehemiah and Ezra to take some dramatic steps. Nehemiah set about ensuring that those who lived in Jerusalem had authentic Jewish parentage (Neh. 7:5f.). In this Nehemiah seemed anxious to achieve racial separation, and no doubt this was considered desirable in order to safeguard the priority of the Jewish religion. Throughout Old Testament times marriage with non-Jews was prohibited, but not on grounds of racial superiority. There were two main reasons for the exclusion of other peoples: historical, and religious or religio-cultural, the latter reason seeming to exercise greater influence. The Ammonites and Moabites were excluded for historical reasons (Deut. 23:4); and for historical reasons the Egyptians were favored (Deut. 23:8); in contrast, marriage with Canaanites was forbidden on religious grounds. Thus Samson's parents questioned the wisdom of his marrying "from the uncircumcised Philistines" (Judg. 14:3). This is not simply an expression of a cultural aversion, for circumcision was at the very heart of the Jewish understanding of the covenant relationship with God. In Ezra's prayer he refers to Yahweh's injunction regarding intermarriage:

Therefore give not your daughters to their sons, and never seek their peace or prosperity, that you may be strong, and eat the good of the land, and leave it for an inheritance to your children for ever. (Ezra 9:12)

The fear was that the Israelites might be enticed away from their traditional faith "to serve other gods" (Deut. 7:14; cf. Judg. 3:6). No wonder that Ezra went to Jerusalem armed with the "statutes and ordinances" of his people and taught them; he had to ensure that his people kept to their religious traditions.

Well after Ezra, in the second century B.C.E., Jewish resentment of Syrian rule came to a head. The Jewish revolt against Antiochus Epiphanes and his successors was in reality a revolt against the attempt to abolish the distinction between the Jews and the Gentiles. When the Syrian monarch proscribed the sabbath observance, circumcision, and so forth, he was in effect proscribing the worship of Yahweh. Not to have resisted was to destroy the ancestral faith, and with it the traditional understanding of the distinctiveness of the Jews.[7]

One could add to the number of episodes in the story of the life and thought of Israel which spell an exclusivist attitude to other peoples and their traditions, but enough has already been said to indicate a triumphalism in the biblical account arising out of the conviction that Israel stood in a special relationship with God. A definite religio-cultural bias is evident, especially where the integrity of Israel as a nation is seen as being at stake. Perhaps, considering the frequency with which Israel was involved in violent confrontations with others, this bias is understandable. Israel's religion was a national religion from the beginning, which would account for this exclusivism.

CONTINUITY BETWEEN ISRAELITE AND OTHER RELIGIONS

Fortunately this is not the only attitude discernible in the Old Testament, for it amounts to theological discontinuity with other peoples' traditions, which suggests a God of limited sovereignty, a view which is challenged in other parts of the Old Testament and also in the New Testament. In much material scattered throughout the Old Testament the thought of a theological continuity between Israel's and other traditions is clearly discernible. Not only did God create humanity,[8] but also when humans repeatedly disobeyed God, God did not cast them off. It is affirmed more than once in Genesis that it is by God's action that the human race is diverse. In the story of the Tower of Babel, human cultural striving is critically viewed, but it becomes clear that while cultural pride is deprecated, cultural development per se is not the object of condemnation. Then comes the promise to Abraham which states, among other things, that by Abraham "all the families of the earth will bless themselves" (Gen. 12:3), which links up with the story of the creation of the human race.[9]

There is much in the Old Testament which seems to issue from the conviction that the human race is one. Many passages speak of all peoples being under God and acting under God's direction. There is, for example, the account of the episode in 701 B.C.E. when Jerusalem was on the verge of being taken by the Assyrians under their king Sennacherib (2 Kings 18-19). A stressful situation such as this was likely to be viewed by the Israelites as indicative of Yahweh's impotence or anger; after all, were they not God's people? The Old Testament makes a determined effort to counter this type of thinking, basing this effort on a broader understanding of the sovereignty of God. Thus with reference to the 701 B.C.E. episode Isaiah speaks of everything having been brought about by Yahweh; indeed, Assyria herself will be punished for her haughtiness after she has successfully carried out God's wishes (2 Kings 19:32ff.; Isa. 10:5-19). In this same episode a high-ranking official of the Assyrian court is presented as saying to King Hezekiah, "Is it without the Lord that I have come up against this place to destroy it?" (2 Kings 18:25). In line with this type of thinking we have Jeremiah's expressed conviction that the taking of Jerusalem by the king of Babylon was Yahweh's doing (Jer. 32:26). Similarly the Persian king Cyrus states that it was "the God of Israel" who had put it into his heart to let the Jewish exiles go (Ezra 1:1f.; cf. 5:13f.). Even if it is allowed that this decree by Cyrus is evidence of a definite theological coloring by the Jewish compilers, it is still of considerable interest because of the broadmindedness it represents; Cyrus is God's anointed (Isa. 45:1f.). Of course, it is known that Cyrus was eclectic in his attitude to religion, as also was his son and successor Cambyses, but this does not detract from the striking nature of the expression of openness. When Jeremiah wrote to the Babylonian exiles advising them to "seek the welfare of the city where I have sent you into exile" (Jer. 29:7) he was being surprisingly accommodating.

Many prophets must have surprised their contemporaries by asserting that Yahweh's own people, as well as the non-Israelite peoples, deserved to be punished by Yahweh. The fact that Israel was Yahweh's own people would not save her from being seriously chastised (Amos 3:2; cf. Deut. 8:19). Amos set out to disabuse the minds of his people regarding their tendency to see "the day of the Lord" (Amos 5:18) as a day of glory for Israel. Popular belief in Israel held that a day was coming when God would wreak vengeance upon Israel's enemies and establish God's rule. Amos says, on the contrary, that that day will be one of gloom, not light; and Isaiah confidently affirms that when that day comes God's anger will be shown, not against enemies but against sinners; there will be a catastrophe which will sweep away evil people, both within and without the covenant community (Isa. 2:12ff.; 13:6-13). Israel is as hardhearted as the non-Israelites and refuses to return.

It must be admitted that this blending together of Israel and the other peoples does sound an exclusivist note, for in the background is the thought that Israel has not been able to keep herself away from the iniquities of the non-Israelite peoples who supremely deserve to be punished. When God has intervened, the world will no longer be a place where people—whether Israelites or non-Israelites—strut arrogantly and perpetrate evil. All the same, the very thought of God's people deserving the treatment that will surely be meted out to other peoples is significant, for it shows that God's special relations with Israel would not stop God from putting righteousness above all other considerations. Indeed, in a sense Israel was even more reprehensible. Ezekiel is told by God that if he were to be sent to "peoples of foreign speech and a hard language, whose words you cannot understand" (Ezek. 3:6), they would repent—but not Israel! Jeremiah in fact taught that the very traditions which Israel treasured so much, such as the temple and its worship, were not indispensable; God would destroy the temple as Shiloh had been destroyed (Jer. 7:1f.).

There is something else which is of fundamental importance: the history of Israel shows that the people were not averse to making use of other peoples' religio-cultural ideas. Having appropriated Canaanite centers of worship it was to be expected that some Canaanite ideas and practices would find their way into Israelite life and thought.[10]

The settlement of the Israelites in Canaan brought them face to face with the religion of its inhabitants, according to which the baals, or the many manifestations of Baal, were the real owners of the land with the power to make agricultural pursuits successful. Several responses were possible in the face of this kind of religion. In the knowledge that none could compare with Yahweh the Israelites could totally reject this kind of religion as being contrary to their covenant relationship with Yahweh. Some of the Israelites did precisely that; as late as the sixth century B.C.E. the Rechabites were distinguished by their refusal to adopt the post-desert structures of life (see Jer. 35). However, even though the Rechabite stand was important as a reminder of the enticements of a settled life in Canaan, it is doubtful whether the Hebrew religious genius revolved around the extremism of the Rechabites. A second response might have been to abandon the worship of Yahweh altogether and adopt Baal worship in its place. The chances are that some Israelites made this response, though it could not have been by any means a popular response. Thirdly, the Israelites could have adopted the fertility cult of the Canaanites in the belief that their prosperity depended on it, while at the same time recognizing Yahweh as the national war god. This could have held much promise as a response for many an Israelite, particularly in the circumstances of the early days of the settlement, but as it turned out it was not the most popular response. It would seem that the response most widely made was to worship Yahweh under the forms of Baal worship.

There was much that was non-Israelite that the Israelites borrowed and worked into their religion, to the enrichment of their traditional life and thought. Canaanite festivals found a place in Israelite worship as a means of expressing the saving acts of God through adaptation and reinterpretation. The Israelite monarchy itself would seem to have resulted from a fusion of Canaanite kingship ideas and the Israelite concept of charismatic leadership as exemplified in the Israelite judges; hence the observation often made that Saul, the first Israelite king,[11] retained the character of a judge. When the prophets used the symbol of the vine and the marriage bond, symbols that dramatize most effectively the relations between God and Israel, they were bearing witness to Israel's indebtedness to Canaan. Indeed, the extent of the use of agricultural imagery by the prophets is quite remarkable. Isaiah in particular furnishes a number of examples, the most memorable of them being the song "for my beloved" (Isa. 5).

The very concept of Yahweh was enriched through this contact with Canaanite life and thought. There were those who called Yahweh Baal in order to emphasize Yahweh's role as the provider of sustenance. Deuteronomic criticism of Canaanite practices is severe, as already noted, and this criticism is echoed by the eighth-century prophet Hosea who views with disfavor the Israelite habit of calling Yahweh Baal: "I will remove the names of the Baals from her mouth, and they shall be mentioned by name no more" (Hos. 2:19). Yet Hosea goes on to say:

> And in that day, says the Lord,
> I will answer the heavens
> and they shall answer the earth;
> and the earth shall answer the grain,
> the wine, and the oil. (Hos. 2:23-24)

When Israel responds to God—and Hosea frequently expresses the hope for a response to God's love, this will give rise to other responses: from the heavens in the falling rain, and from the earth in the vine and the fruit. In other words, Yahweh is to provide those very things which some Israelites, through contact with the Canaanites, had come to expect from the baals. Thus were the expectations of Israel sanctified. It is worth emphasizing that Hosea does not reject the earthly hopes and desires of his people, reminiscent though they were of the Israelite contact with the Canaanites; these hopes and desires are deemed valid but they are recontextualized, so that it is now Yahweh who fulfils them.

It was in the early monarchy, in particular, that much assimilation of non-Israelite ideas and practices took place, though the process had, of course, started much earlier. Israelite wisdom, for example, owed much to the wisdom traditions of other peoples. There are a number of biblical references to wisdom and wise men of the ancient world; thus the wise men of Egypt (1 Kings 4:30; Isa. 19:11, 12; Acts 7:22), Edom (Jer. 49:7; Obad. 8), and Phoenicia (Ezek. 28:1f., Zech. 9:2) are spoken of, often with respect. Israel might not have taken to Egyptian polytheistic systems, but she was not averse to borrowing from Egyptian wisdom literature. The Egyptian *Teaching of Ptahhotep* is quite ancient, dating from 2450 B.C.E. Perhaps a better known Egyptian wisdom work is *The Teaching of Amenemope* which is probably to be dated about the time of the Israelite judges, or even earlier; this work is generally acknowledged to have influenced the compilation of the Book of Proverbs.

The Israelites might have been averse to bringing Yahweh down to the level of the many gods in the ancient world, but the development of their understanding of Yahweh was in certain respects shaped in interaction with their neighbors in the ancient world. Thus Solomon's temple was fashioned after a Phoenician temple; indeed, there was a tradition that the Jerusalem temple was to serve as a universal inspiration for all nations. This may be illustrated by reference to the prophecies of Isaiah in the eighth century, a period of Israelite history when hostile forces threatened and finally overcame Samaria. The prophet looks into the future, uttering the words:

> It shall come to pass in the latter days
>> that the mountain of the house of the Lord
> shall be established as the highest of the mountains,
>> and shall be raised above the hills;
> and all the nations shall flow to it,
>> and many peoples shall come in, and say:

"Come, let us go up to the mountain of the Lord,
to the house of the God of Jacob." (Isa. 2:2-3)

Similarly, Zechariah foresees a time when "everyone that survives of all the nations that have come against Jerusalem shall go up year after year to worship the King, the Lord of hosts, and to keep the feast of booth" (Zech. 14:16).

MALACHI AND ISRAEL'S RELATION WITH THE WORLD

In the light of sentiments such as these, some of the prophecies of Malachi gain in interest, and deserve something more than a cursory glance, for they contain suggestions of a wrestling with the issue of the relation between Israel and the world. The prophet's words are full of feeling. The reader soon becomes conscious of the prophet's critical attitude toward the religious life of the people. There was evidently an internal crisis in the Jerusalem community of the fifth century B.C.E. More than half of this collection of prophecies is devoted to a criticism of the Jews for their disregard of the laws of God: the people were grossly careless in the fulfillment of their cultic duties; worshipers and priests alike were defaulting in their duty to God; blemished animals were being presented and offered in God's house; the payment of tithes was being withheld; and the cult was becoming increasingly external. The priests also were criticized for their lifestyle and teaching; evidently they had come to look upon the cult simply as a source of income. Thus the worship which was carried on in the temple was so deficient that the prophet expressed the wish that someone would "shut the doors, that you might not kindle fire upon my altar in vain!" (Mal. 1:10).

Despite Malachi's criticisms, however, it is clear that he remains firmly attached to the traditions of his people. Thus he speaks with approval of Levi, the covenant with whom was "of life and peace, and I gave them to him, that he might fear; and he feared me, he stood in awe of my name" (Mal. 2:5). Thus not only does he endorse the tradition regarding the setting aside of the house of Levi for the priesthood, but also he finds that what the priests of his day were doing was a corruption of that covenant. After all, to be a priest one must show evidence of the right kind of genealogical descent; it was for that reason that in the post-exilic community certain people were excluded from the priesthood—they had unacceptable ancestry (Ezra 2:61-63; Neh. 7:63-65). In this connection the prophet's criticism of divorce is of interest (Mal. 2:10-16), for it is prefaced with the wider implications of mixed marriages: marriage with foreigners is a demonstration of infidelity to God's covenant with the people. To Malachi it was regrettable that those who were firmly associated with Israel by their ancestry, and thus part of the covenant, should behave in flagrant disregard of the tradition of Israel's special link with God.

Malachi's criticisms, then, contain a hint of regret; he evidently wished that his people, including the priests, would show a commitment to the covenant. He is in effect appealing to his people to reconsider; hence his words, "So take heed to yourselves and do not be faithless" (Mal. 2:16).

It is precisely because of his desire to maintain tradition that the prophet's references to the nations startle and call for an explanation. In 1:5 he declares, "Great is the Lord, beyond the borders of Israel!" This declaration reveals Malachi's firm conviction that God's sovereignty extends beyond Israel; his "name is feared among the nations" (Mal. 1:14). This conviction is exemplified in two ways. First, Edom had thought, quite erroneously, that she could ignore God's anger. The historical episode underlying this reference cannot be determined with any certainty, and perhaps it is unnecessary to endeavor to identify the exact historical circumstances alluded to. What is important is the recognition of Yahweh's freedom to exercise power where Yahweh wills. That this was not a new thought is readily recognized; such a thought had been expressed by the prophets before Malachi, such as Jeremiah in his letter to the Babylonian exiles (Jer. 29:1-28), and Deutero-Isaiah in the conviction that God ordered events outside Palestine (Isa. 45:1f.).

The second exemplification is somewhat startling and has been the subject of a variety of speculations. The prophet proclaims:

For from the rising of the sun to its setting my name is great among the nations, and in every place incense is

offered to my name, and a pure offering; for my name is
great among the nations, says the Lord of hosts. (Mal. 1:11)

The phrase "from the rising of the sun to its setting" could mean
either "all the world over" or "from dawn to dusk." The reference to "nations" would seem to imply that the prophet is
speaking of what goes on the world over, though quite possibly
the two meanings of the reference to the rising and setting of
the sun are intended to operate at once: the greatness of God's
name is recognized in all places and at all times.

The next question is whether or not the prophet had some
identifiable people or peoples in mind. It has been suggested,
for example, that he had in mind the Jews of the diaspora and
is commending the worship activity of the Jews "at Elephantine,
for instance, and perhaps at Kasiphia in Babylonia."[12] In this
understanding "nations" refers to the peoples among whom
Jewish settlements were to be found, and "place" means the
sanctuary (see Deut. 12:5). It has been argued that if this interpretation were correct it would show a curious departure from
"Deuteronomic orthodoxy, of which the first essential was that
the Temple at Jerusalem should have a monopoly of worship."[13]
It has been pointed out, however, that even though the Jews of
the dispersion could not offer sacrifice, the temple in Jerusalem
being the only legitimate place for it, yet there was nothing to
stop them from commemorating the feasts and fasts. In any case,
according to this interpretation God finds acceptable the worship carried out by diaspora Jews because it is truer than that
carried out by the Jews in Jerusalem.

This does not seem to be a very likely interpretation, from
what is known of Jewish worship at Elephantine, for example,
where both Yahweh and a consort seem to have been recognized; in any case, it does not appear to be the most natural
interpretation. Precisely because the prophet excoriates his people for disregarding the traditions of the ancestors, it is much
more likely that the contrast intended by the prophet does not
refer to the Jews of the diaspora; the plain sense of the prophet's
words implies a sharper contrast.

Is it not possible that the prophet is saying that the worship
of the nations at large will be found more acceptable than the

worship activity going on in Jerusalem? The fifth century B.C.E. was a time when the Jews lived in close proximity with non-Jews. At that time Judah was not much larger than Jerusalem and its immediate environs as chunks of the land had been seized by some of the neighboring peoples from whom the Jews suffered repeated attacks.[14] There was considerable resentment, but perhaps it was Judah's very vulnerability which contributed to the broadmindedness voiced by Malachi, and which became characteristic of post-exilic days in certain circles.[15]

Assuming, then, that the heathen are in mind, is it possible to characterize the intended significance even more closely? There are two possible ways of proceeding: it is either that the gods of the heathen are to be recognized as the one God (a universal monotheism), or that the worship of the heathen is acceptable before Yahweh because it is more sincere. The former is the view expressed by Isaiah, as already noted;[16] Isaiah is seeking to abolish distinctions—there will be only one form of worship for all the nations. Malachi, in contrast, is not out to abolish distinctions; his position appears much more intriguing than Isaiah's. Malachi's vision is of a world in which the worship practices of the different religions, if sincere, deserve respect as a commitment to deity.

It may be wondered whether, in view of Malachi's strong desire for his people to respect their own traditions, the interpretation given here of his words is plausible. It is worth pointing out that the prophet is not making a theoretical assessment of religions. It is from the starting point of the corrupt worship of his people that he suggests that sincere worship, even if it is by non-Jews, is preferable. In view of this it is pointless to ask whether he would have spoken with approval of non-Jewish worship if Jewish worship had been sincere. What is a fact is that instead of rejecting non-Jewish worship out of hand he applauds it.

These then are the two attitudes—the exclusivist and the open—which exist side by side in the Old Testament; no attempt is made to reconcile them. Considering the strong nationalistic spirit evident in the exclusivist attitude, it is perhaps remarkable that the open attitude finds expression at all. This open attitude is expressed basically in terms of God's grace being available for all peoples, though the thought assumes two contrasting forms. According to one, the nations are acceptable to God in and through their own traditions, and according to the other, all peoples shall recognize and acknowledge in worship the God of Israel.

NON-JEWS AND THE COVENANT

In this connection there is more to be said about the Old Testament. If indeed it was hoped that other peoples would come to worship Yahweh, how, in practice, was this inclusiveness understood? In view of the material to be surveyed in the second chapter, it is necessary to explore how Jewish tradition viewed the place of non-Jews in the context of the covenant tradition.

To begin with, it would seem that initially the idea of religious conversion was not part of the Israelite tradition. Non-Israelites who settled in Israel would in the course of time be permitted to become part of the Israelite community: "The children of the third generation that are born to them may enter the assembly of the Lord" (Deut. 23:9). As a matter of fact, foreign ethnic groups could be incorporated into Israel with their ethnic identities intact. Examples of such groups are the Midianites, descended from Moses' father-in-law (Num. 10:29ff.) and the Gibeonites (Josh. 9:1ff.). The descendants of Moses' father-in-law were so much part of Israel that Jael, the wife of Heber the Kenite,[17] could gladly eliminate Sisera, the Canaanite chieftain who had threatened Israel's peace (Judg. 4:17ff.); and the Gibeonites became Israelites in religion.

Thus from the beginning non-Israelites could share in the Torah; strangers or sojourners were to observe the feast of the unleavened bread (Exod. 12:19) and the law of the sabbath rest (Lev. 16:29); and the stranger who failed to observe the law regarding the eating of blood "shall bear his iniquity" (Lev. 17:16). As the Book of Exodus puts it, "There shall be one law for the native and for the stranger who sojourns among you" (Exod. 12:49). Indeed, "the sojourner who is in your camp, both he who hews your wood and he who draws your water" may with the rest of Israel "enter into the sworn covenant of the Lord your God, which the Lord your God makes with you this day" (Deut. 29:11-12). When Joshua assembled the Israelites and wrote a copy of the law of Moses he read this "before all the assembly of Israel, and the women, and the little ones, and the sojourners who lived among them" (Josh. 8:35). In this connection part of the prayer of dedication made by King Solomon is of interest:

> Likewise when a foreigner, who is not of thy people Israel, comes from a far country for thy name's sake (for they shall hear of thy great name, and thy mighty hand, and of thy outstretched arm), when he comes and prays toward this house, hear thou in heaven thy dwelling place, and do according to all for which the foreigner calls to thee. (1 Kings 8:41-43)

All this represents a striking broadmindedness, even though the attitude thus made explicit does not involve abandoning all that the Israelites held dear. Considering the centrality of circumcision in the traditions of Israel it is not surprising that it was stipulated that a stranger could participate in the Passover celebration only after undergoing circumcision (Exod. 12:48-49).

So far it has been a matter of the Israelites giving sojourners the right to be part of the religious community, insofar as this inclusion was possible without injury to the Israelite traditions. The instances cited above are not religious conversion as such; they are simply what has been described as permissible religious inclusion.

As far as religious conversion is concerned, Kaufmann sees in the story of Naaman the "seeds" of such conversion.[18] However that may be, it is the only clear Old Testament reference to the Israelite faith being consciously adopted by a foreigner with the intention of practicing it back in his own country. It was in much later times, during the Second Temple period, that the desire to take the Jewish religion beyond the borders of Palestine assumed serious proportions and led to the institution of proselytism. To be sure, particularistic tendencies predominated, especially in Palestinian Judaism, but the more open tendencies flourished. There was a great deal of eagerness to make converts, the Jews seeing themselves as "a light to the nations, that my salvation may reach to the end of the earth" (Isa. 49:6). That a great deal of success was achieved in this regard is testified to by the Jewish historian Josephus who wrote:

> The masses have long since shown a keen desire to adopt our religious observances; and there is not one city, Greek or barbarian, nor a single nation, to which our custom of abstaining from work on the seventh day has not spread, and where the fasts and the lighting of lamps and many of our prohibitions in the matter of food are not observed.[19]

It would seem that the non-Jews who attached themselves to the Jewish faith were categorized as either God-fearers or proselytes. The existence of the category of God-fearers has been questioned, the term being seen by some as a general description of observing non-Jews. However, the evidence seems to argue in favor of such a category of believers who, having been attracted by the Jewish religious life, attended Jewish synagogues without adhering to all the laws of Judaism. Consequently they were not considered to be fully part of the community of faith (see Acts 13:16, 26, 43; 17:4, 17). The proselytes, on the other hand, were regarded as an integral part of the community of faith, being expected to observe the whole Torah; in particular, they were to observe the rite of circumcision, undergo baptism (purificatory immersion), and to take an offering to the sanctuary. However, even though proselytes, unlike God-fearers, had to adopt Judaism in its entirety, they "might never call the ancestors of Israel (their) fathers."[20] Furthermore, it was not unknown for non-Jewish converts to Judaism to adopt a Hebrew name.[21] Whether this was demanded, or whether the converts themselves felt that this was an appropriate step in view of their new status, such adoption indicates the total nature of the demand which Judaism made on its converts.

Up till the time of Christ, then, Judaism was a religion which deeply treasured its traditions, so much so that though some passionately believed that the faith must be taken beyond the borders of Palestine, there was a great concern for not sacrificing the character of the faith in the process. Jesus expressed this when he said:

Woe to you, scribes and Pharisees, hypocrites! for you traverse sea and land to make a single proselyte, and when he becomes a proselyte, you make him twice as much a child of hell as yourselves. (Matt. 23:15)

2

The Early Church:
Questions and Attitudes

The Old Testament, with its lack of a uniform attitude toward other peoples and their traditions, was the foundation document of the church when it came into being following the death and resurrection of Christ. Immediately, then, the question arises of the extent to which the attitudes surveyed in the previous chapter shaped the early church's understanding and prosecution of mission. The fact needs to be underlined that the Old Testament meant a great deal to the Jews of the time of Jesus, and to the early church. Israel was a covenant community based on God's acts in history. It was God who brought her out of slavery in Egypt, gave her the land of Canaan, and raised up men and women who were enabled by God to be leaders. Thus the ties that bound God and Israel together had deep roots in history. In the circumstances, therefore, Israel's continued existence was seen to be dependent upon her remembering that history in which God had played such a pivotal role, and on her being loyal to God. Deuteronomy's call to the people to remember their past and how it was shaped by God, and to look upon the present as being inseparably linked to the past (Deut. 26:5-10), was one that continued to ring in the ears of the faithful. Given the nature of their national history, the Jews in the time of Jesus and in the early church lived not simply by God's guidance as they experienced it in their own time, but also by their roots, especially as found in the Old Testament which were the only Scriptures for those Jews who were loyal to their past. The Scriptures were a guide to the Jewish community in all spheres; they were meant to be read in public gatherings for worship in temple and synagogue, and their demands were observed in the home where circumcision took place, and where the Passover meal was eaten.

As already shown, attitudes toward other peoples and their traditions constitute a significant element in the Old Testament and, it must be presumed, exercised some influence as the Jews sought to relate to non-Jews. That the early church wrestled with the concept of mission is clearly evidenced in the New Testament records. It will be seen presently that the New Testament, like the Old, does not display a uniform attitude toward pagan peoples. Thus the biblical record as a whole does not speak with one voice regarding the attitude to be adopted toward people of other faiths. It is this record which influenced many to go out into unknown and often hazardous situations which shaped their preaching and missionary strategy. It is not suprising, therefore, that uncertainties are reflected in the modern missionary enterprise, as will be shown subsequently.

I propose, then, to begin by looking at the early church's missionary endeavors as reflected in the New Testament. It will be necessary, however, to preface this with a brief examination of the life and teaching of Jesus, having in mind attitudes toward other peoples and their life and thought.

THE GOSPELS: JEWISH TRADITION AND ATTITUDES TOWARD GENTILES

It must be stated at the outset that Jesus accepted that the Jewish religious traditions had much validity. If there was one element in Judaism which its adherents considered to be most central it was the *Shema*: "Hear, O Israel: The Lord our God is one Lord" (Deut. 6:4). Jesus quotes this with approval (Mark 12:29). It is perhaps significant that Mark recalls this conviction in response to a question put to Jesus by one of the scribes, the theological experts. In quoting the *Shema* Jesus shows that he shares the concern of the scribes for recognising that this affirmation is the basis of the Jewish faith. Furthermore, Jesus shared the view, inherent in the Decalogue, that the primacy of God must influence interpersonal relationships (Mark 10:17-19; Exod. 20:1ff.). It is also made clear in the gospel accounts that on more than one occasion Jesus showed his willingness to accept Jewish customs as valid, as when he advised the cured leper to show himself to the priest for certification purposes (Mark 1:40-44), and endorsed the tradition concerning the return of Elijah (Mark 9:9-13). Indeed, in Jesus the traditions of Judaism were seen to be fulfilled: Moses and Elijah appear with him at his transfiguration (Mark 9:2-8), and he is seen as the son of David, the Messianic figure (Mark 10:47, 11:10), and as Elijah *redivivus* (Mark 6:15).

Thus the gospels, whether by what Jesus himself said or did or by others' perception of him and his role, endorse the traditions of Judaism.

This is only one aspect of the matter, however, for sometimes in the process of endorsing a Jewish custom Jesus would in fact depart from it. Thus when he was asked about divorce he not only recognized the validity of the teaching of Moses in its own context, but also went further than that tradition when he said, "Whoever divorces his wife and marries another, commits adultery against her" (Mark 10:2-12). In fact, on a number of occasions he set aside Jewish traditions altogether: he acted in contravention of the sabbath law (Mark 2:23-28), disregarded Jewish scruples relating to ceremonial cleanness (Mark 1:40-41, 7:1-15), and taught, no doubt to the utter dismay of his Jewish audiences, that the Jews were no better than the Gentiles (Mark 12:1-14).

In the light of the references just made, two episodes in the life and teaching of Jesus call for a comment. The baptism of Jesus could not have endeared Jesus to his people, for they were being invited to undergo a rite by which Gentiles were made proselytes (Mark 1:9-11). Jesus' baptism was, among other things, a powerful symbol of his sense of solidarity with the Gentiles. The second episode is the cleansing of the temple (Mark 11:15-17). On that occasion Jesus, quoting Isaiah (Isa.

56:7), said, "My house shall be called a house of prayer for all the nations." At first sight these words do not seem to be a direct response to the occasion, but it may be noted that the commercial activity to which Jesus so strongly objected was centered in the Court of the Gentiles, the only place in the temple which was open to those non-Jews who had developed an interest in Judaism. It may be assumed that all that commercial preoccupation had meant that there was little or no space for the Gentiles in the temple.

The Jewish author of the Gospel of Matthew gives us reason to believe that the Jewish attitude to the Gentiles could be quite uncomplimentary. The Gentiles are likened to dogs or swine (Matt. 7:6), and their way of life is criticized because it is opposed to that of the Jews who know God as Father (Matt. 6:7-8). Their manner of social interaction (Matt. 5:47), their mode of prayer (Matt. 6:7), their attitude to power (Matt. 20:25)—all these are criticized by Jesus. Indeed, it is the Gentiles who are the ones to whom Jesus will be handed over, and who will maltreat and execute him (Matt. 22:19); the disciples themselves are not going to escape the hatred of the Gentiles (Matt. 10:18). If there is a verse which most strikingly sums up the uncomplimentary attitude to the Gentiles, it is, "If [your brother] refused to listen to them, tell it to the church; and if he refuses to listen to the church, let him be to you as a Gentile and a tax collector" (Matt. 18:17).

Jesus shows hardly any knowledge of pagan religion. He did not, of course, leave Gentile areas out of his itinerary (see Mark 7:24-37). In this connection a distinction has sometimes been drawn between the mission of the Twelve and that of the Seventy. The former has been seen as a mission to the Jews; Matthew specifically notes that the Twelve were forbidden to go anywhere among the Gentiles (Matt. 10:5). The gospel accounts of this mission do not present it as a resounding success. Luke's account of the mission of the Seventy, on the other hand, has been taken to be that of a Gentile mission, the number seventy is believed to recall the supposed seventy nations of the world (Gen. 10), and Luke specifically notes that it was a successful mission.[1] However that may be, Jesus did preach in Gentile areas also, and probably achieved a certain measure of success, as may be deduced from what he said in reaction to the centurion's demonstration of faith: "Many will come from east and west and sit at table with Abraham, Isaac, and Jacob in the kingdom of heaven, while the sons of the kingdom will be thrown into the outer darkness" (Matt. 8:11-12).

It may be wondered, however, whether Jesus in fact considered a mission to the Gentiles to be urgent. The Syrophoenician woman responded to Jesus' apparent reluctance to accede to her request in the words: "Yes, Lord; yet even the dogs under the table eat the children's crumbs" (Mark 7:24-30). In these words the anxious Gentile parent was acknowledging Jesus' special concern for his people. Was Jesus unwilling to divert his attention from his own people in order to help a non-Jew?

Incidentally, Luke's interests are such that he endeavors to eliminate those expressions which seem to spell contempt for the Gentiles; further, he introduces episodes which show most strikingly Jesus' good relations with non-Jews. Thus Luke omits Mark 7:27, and describes how when Jesus' disciples wanted to call down fire from heaven to consume the Samaritans Jesus stopped them (Luke 9:51-56). The parable of the Good Samaritan is aimed at negating the Jewish distaste for non-Jews (Luke 10:29-37). In fact, Luke's writings represent a "reinterpretation of the gospel within the context of a pluralistic environment composed of both Jews and Gentiles."[2]

To go back to Jesus' encounter with the Syrophoenician woman, the truth of the matter seems to be that Jesus did not see a mission to the Gentiles with the same sense of urgency as he saw a mission to his own people, against the background of whose traditions he had come as the Messiah. He evidently wanted to start among the Jews, and thus create a foundation for formally launching the Gentile mission.[3] And the church, when it came into being, understood from Jesus' life and teaching that his followers were to "go . . . and make disciples of all the nations" (Matt. 28:19). Indeed, John's gospel begins with what may be looked upon as a counterpart of the Old Testament creation story:

In the beginning was the Word, and the Word was with God, and the Word was God. He was in the beginning with

God; all things were made through him, and without him
was not anything made that was made. (John 1:1-3)

The Word of God was the agent in the creation of the world,
so that human life is related to God through its creation and
illumination by God's Word.

Jesus, then, was not prepared to accept the Jewish traditions
uncritically, even though he acknowledged that they had a place
in a person's relationship with God. Though he might not have
viewed a Gentile mission with a sense of urgency, he nevertheless considered Gentiles to be as deserving of God's attention
as the Jews.

In the biblical documents which deal more directly with the
life and thought of the early church we find much more detailed
impressions of how the church's Jewish background was seen to
bear upon the Gentile outreach. For our study of the early
church's missionary efforts it will be sufficient to cite three main
New Testament sources, The Acts of the Apostles, Paul's Letter
to the Galatians, and his first Letter to the Corinthians, though
this chapter will focus on the first two. The Acts of the Apostles
and Galatians may be described as "contemporary" documents
for the simple reason that they deal for the most part with issues
concerned with the missionary drive into non-Jewish areas. With
non-Jews being converted to Christianity the issue arose as to
what kind of lifestyle would best witness to the converts' new
status. It soon became evident that in endeavoring to face this
issue the early church was divided; tensions arose in the community of Christians over the opening of the church's doors to
the Gentiles.

In this chapter, then, attention will be paid to those two
books, having in mind certain questions: Does the New Testament give evidence of serious thinking on the subject of missions? And to what extent does the New Testament reflect the
issue of continuity between the Word of God and the traditions
of other peoples?

MISSION IN THE ACTS OF THE APOSTLES

It may be noted, to begin with, that The Acts of the Apostles
seems to have been written, at least in part, to show that the

gospel does not present any insuperable barrier to the non-Jew. Not only does it note that Paul's first convert as an evangelist was a Roman official (Acts 13:12), but also Paul is made to assert, almost as the last words of the book, "Let it be known to you then that this salvation of God has been sent to the Gentiles; they will listen" (Acts 28:28). Luke seems to have carefully mapped out the story on the basis of the resources available to him, and presents the drive among the Gentiles as an unavoidable part of the church's task. It is also evident—and Luke's account does give indications of the tensions that existed in the church—that the Gentile drive laid bare the strengths and weaknesses of the church's understanding of its task. In this connection the Stephen episode is instructive.

The sixth chapter of The Acts deals with the story of the appointment of the seven "deacons" who were to oversee the work of the distribution of alms in the church in the days of the apostles. This episode reflects the tensions that the church began to experience when Jews who had been brought up in the Greek world joined the Jewish Christians in the church. But there is more to the episode and a closer look at the story discloses some instructive sidelights. Thus it is of interest that the problem of the distribution of alms arose in the first place. There were both Hebrews and Hellenists in the church. The latter term is often said to be a description of Greek-speaking Jews, but it has been pointed out that though the Jews in question might have been Greek-speaking, the term indicated more generally those Jews who were prepared to accommodate Greek ways of life, in contrast to the Hebrews who were the conservative Palestinian Jews.[4] Perhaps before the widows of those Hellenistic Jews joined the Christian church, they had been receiving help from the temple treasury. If so, then their new religious affiliation made them beneficiaries of the church's largesse. New Testament sources (see 1 Tim. 5:3,9,16) and the church Fathers witness to the fact that widows received recognition and material help from the church.

It is tempting to ask the question: Was the neglect of the Hellenistic widows by the Hebrews deliberate? This would not be an altogether idle question, however. Quite possibly an influx of Hellenistic widows had begun to strain the church's resources and was progressively reducing what the Hebrew widows had come to consider as their entitlement, resulting in a certain amount of ill feeling. In addition, the Hellenistic widows were probably looked upon as having less than adequate Jewish credentials anyway. Was there a chink in the church's communalistic armor?[5]

The seven were duly elected. There may be nothing in the fact that they all bore Greek names; Palestinian Jews were not beyond taking Greek names.[6] In fact we are told specifically that only Nicolaus was a proselyte (Acts 6:5). This, of course, does not remove the uncertainty surrounding the cultural background of the other six, for it is not by any means certain that the pointed description of Nicolaus implies that the others were not proselytes. Quite probably, however, they were all Hellenistic Jews. At any rate, it is to be assumed that they were broadminded Christians, even though we have practically no information about four of them beyond their appointment on this occasion. We know that Philip brought the Ethiopian eunuch to faith in Christ (Acts 8:26f.) and Stephen was killed for his views on Jewish traditions. Nicolaus, we are told by Irenaeus,[7] was the founder of the Nicolaitans, a group which was considered heretical (Rev. 2:6). Little is otherwise known about this group, but probably it drew criticism for adopting a nonconservative outlook.[8] Furthermore, it is not without significance that Nicolaus is associated with Antioch, for at Antioch, according to Josephus, many Greeks had been attracted to the worship of the Jews and joined them.[9] This town, one strongly suspects, assumed a great deal of importance in the early church even though Jerusalem is made to overshadow every other center of activity. There is a strong possibility, from several indications in The Acts, that a definite policy of going to the Gentiles was first adopted at Antioch.

If it is doubted that the church would elect only Hellenists to fill the position of "deacon," there are other considerations which lend support to the possibility of the seven having been all, or at least preponderantly, Hellenists. A fact of some significance is that some of the seven acted more like evangelists than administrators. Quite possibly the matter of the distribution of alms only served to bring to a head an already festering cleavage between the Palestinian Jews and the Hellenistic Jews on the issue of the treatment of non-Jews seeking church membership. This would make the so-called deacons the leaders to whom the Hellenists would look for both material and spiritual help, just as the Palestinian Jews would look up to the apostles. That there were opposing viewpoints in the church can hardly be a matter for doubt.

STEPHEN'S VIEWS ON JEWISH TRADITIONS

The situation was in fact somewhat more complicated, for it would seem that there were "parties" among the Hellenistic Jews themselves. Stephen engaged the Hellenistic Jews in discussion in their synagogues on how much weight should be placed on Jewish traditions. If he had expected to receive support for his views he was sadly disappointed, for the Hellenists, worsted in the debate with Stephen, instigated charges against him (Acts 6:9f.). Apparently some of the Hellenists were so close to the "conservatives" that they felt that their Jewish traditions were being threatened by his preaching. They wanted to be open, but they were apprehensive regarding where this might lead. It is not necessary to speculate about whether or not these accusing Hellenists were themselves incited by the Sanhedrin members. The Hellenists were evidently conservative enough to believe that Stephen's ideas had the potential to weaken the church's links with the traditions of the patriarchs.

The divisions in the early church, then, arose out of differing attitudes to the issue of continuity, essentially: Is there a continuity between the church's Jewish and non-Jewish traditions? How is this continuity to be conceived, if it exists? To some Jewish Christians—and these would seem to have been in the majority—continuity was conceivable only if the Gentiles adopted Jewish customs. There could not be a continuity which endorsed non-Jewish ways at the expense of Jewish traditions. This is where Stephen's address comes up for consideration.

Stephen was accused of having taught that Jesus would destroy the temple and change the customs which Moses gave the Jews (6:14; cf. Mark 14:58). Luke puts a long address in the mouth of Stephen (Acts 7:2-53)[10] which purports to counter the charges leveled against him. Actually, however, the rebuttal is very indirect. The address makes basically three points: God had dealings with the patriarchs outside the Holy Lands; from the beginning the Jews had frequently rejected those who had been appointed by God to bring them relief; and, the temple could not be considered indispensable since the Old Testament says it was unnecessary, and in any case the tabernacle preceded it. That the address is an attack on Jewish conservatism is clear: Stephen argues, in effect, that God is free to act outside the traditional institutions.[11] This clearly implies that Christianity cannot be tied too closely to Jewish traditions, and by this Stephen drove a wedge between Judaism and Christianity. In contrast, Stephen's accusers could not detach Christianity from Jewish culture.

To be sure, Stephen does not write off the law as unimportant, and in this connection an interesting element in this address may be noted. Much of it is devoted to *the attitude of the Jews toward their own tradition*[12] — the Jews were often disobedient, ignoring the law as the Word of God. If Stephen was being accused of teaching that the law was of no account, then his rebuttal would seem to be: It is the Jews themselves who have mindlessly set aside the law, and it is wrong, in any case, to presume that God is bound to the law in the sense of being enslaved by it. The first of these two countercharges is not a blanket endorsement of tradition (the second makes that clear), nor is the second an invitation to set aside tradition as such. In effect Stephen is saying that tradition should be judiciously used, to free rather than to enslave.

Stephen, then, we might say, would acknowledge a continuity between Jewish tradition and the life and thought of non-Jews who, he would have insisted, did not need to adopt the Jewish way of life as a mark of their having become members of the church.

The violent elimination of Stephen did not stop some of the Christians from taking the message of Christ to non-Jews, though there would have been some hesitation on the part of those who were inclined toward Stephen's way of thinking. Philip went to work among the Samaritans (Acts 8:4ff.) who, well before the Christian era, had separated themselves from the Jews and built their own temple on Mount Gerizim, having adopted a canon of Scripture that differed from the Jewish canon. Philip also encountered the Ethiopian eunuch and baptized him (Acts 8:26-38). Then there is the episode of Peter in the house of Cornelius, the issue at stake being whether or not Peter should neglect the traditions in which he had been nurtured as a Jew and cease to make distinctions between clean and unclean (Acts 10, 11:1-18). Later, back in Jerusalem from Caesarea, Peter was questioned by "the circumcision party" about what had transpired in the house of Cornelius. According to the biblical account, when they heard Peter's account "they were silenced. And they glorified God, saying, 'Then to the Gentiles also God has granted repentance unto life.'" Peter acted as directed by God at that moment. Can it be said that the episode witnesses to Peter's adoption of a circumcisionless Christianity? Apparently not, as Paul's Letter to the Galatians makes clear.

These incidents show that there were some in the early church, in the days of the apostles, who firmly believed that there was no barrier to Gentiles coming into the church. However, at the same time it should be observed that no policy decision had been taken as yet to give guidance to either those who were convinced that the church was right in opening its doors to the Gentiles, or those who would want to see the Gentile drive abandoned altogether or at least hedged about with such precautionary measures as would ensure the preservation of its Jewish background. Quite clearly Jerusalem was divided on the issue of mission to the Gentiles following Stephen's death. Luke's note that "the circumcision party" rejoiced when Peter made his explanations is supported by the fact that "the apostles at Jerusalem" did not hesitate to send Peter and John to Samaria following Philip's activities there, but this is to be set against Luke's other statement:

Now those who were scattered because of the persecution that arose over Stephen travelled as far as Phoenicia and Cyprus and Antioch, speaking the word to none except Jews. (Acts 11:19)

On this tension Paul is perhaps more explicit. Just as Paul felt he had no alternative but to preach to the Gentiles, so there were those, notably Peter, who came to see themselves as "entrusted with the gospel to the circumcised" (Gal. 2:7).

The conclusion is unavoidable that the encounters with the Gentiles in the time of the apostles were incidental and uncoordinated, with no detailed policy decision on the subject by the church with its base at Jerusalem.

THE ROLE OF ANTIOCH

A matter of some interest is that in the story of The Acts the Twelve appear to play a rather limited role; beyond their mention in connection with Jerusalem, most of them receive no individual mention whatsoever. Peter, of course, was actively engaged in preaching. With John at his side he preached among the people of Samaria. He was to arouse controversy over the baptism of Cornelius and his household. Indeed, on the evidence of Paul, Peter was a busy itinerant preacher (1 Cor. 9:5). It is significant, however, that he seemed to have preached more to his own people than to the Gentiles. It is not certain how one explains this apparent inactivity on the part of the Twelve to preach to the Gentiles; had they failed to look beyond the command not to go among the Gentiles (Matt. 10:5)? While one cannot entirely rule out the possibility of their having been more active than they are pictured by Luke, it seems much more likely that the greater part of the evangelistic activity undertaken in those early days was by others than the Twelve. It is tempting to see the explanation lying in the need felt by the Twelve to be in Jerusalem to oversee the needs of the church from the center, but there is probably a better explanation than this. Those who would undertake serious evangelistic work in Palestine at that time would need to know the Greek language as well. The changing cultural face of Palestine meant that it was necessary to employ Greek in order to reach those who had come under the influence of Hellenistic culture. The mother tongue of the Twelve was Aramaic, and though at least some of them must have known the Greek language, those who were best placed to preach to the Greek-speaking peoples were the Hellenistic Jewish Christians, such as Barnabas. Hence the choice of the seven "deacons" who were probably all Hellenistic Jews, and hence the role played by Antioch in the story of the early church.

If we had access to more detailed information on the life of the early church, we would probably find that Antioch assumed considerable importance, perhaps greater importance than Jerusalem—despite the fact that the apostles were in Jerusalem—in the matter of the church's Gentile outreach. In The Acts Luke writes about a time when Jerusalem was the official center of the church; after all, it was the place where the church came into being at Pentecost. In the circumstances he is obliged to focus attention on Jerusalem. If he had not felt that constraint Luke would undoubtedly have told us a great deal more about Antioch and the importance it assumed in those days. In fact there are some indications in the present account which point to the possibility of Antioch having played a significant role. Following the death of Stephen some Jewish Christians preached only to Jews wherever they went, while at Antioch "men of Cyprus and Cyrene ... spoke to the Greeks also, preaching the Lord Jesus. And the hand of the Lord was with them, and a great number that believed turned to the Lord" (Acts 11:20-21). We are evidently meant to understand that those evangelists at Antioch were Greek-speaking Jewish Christians who were no doubt more inclined to see their new faith in a broader perspective than the Palestinian Jewish Christians. We have already noted Josephus' report that at Antioch many Greeks were attracted to the worship of the Jews and joined them. In the church at Antioch, therefore, a more relaxed attitude to Jewish traditions seems to have prevailed. At any rate, when news of events at Antioch reached Jerusalem Barnabas was sent there to bring a report on what was happening. That Jerusalem had the right to oversee what was going on in the church outside the center was not in dispute; however, Antioch would seem to have become the place where the church dared most to relate to Hellenists and non-Jews. It was at Antioch that Paul and Barnabas were set apart for missionary work (Acts 13:1f.), and it was there that the so-called Judaisers came and preached their gospel of circumcision (Acts 15:1f.). There is some indication in all these incidents that it was at Antioch that a definite policy of going to the Gentiles was enunciated and embarked upon, and it was here that the disciples were called Christians for the first time (Acts 11:26).[13] The Acts has been described as a tale of two cities, Jerusalem and Rome,[14] but it is more a tale of three cities, given the crucial nature of the role played by Antioch.

Undoubtedly some Jewish Christians would have had strong reservations about the Antiochean policy, as Paul's first evangelistic tour shows. When Paul, accompanied by Barnabas, arrived at Antioch, he addressed both Jews and those Gentiles who were sympathetic to the Jewish faith (Acts 13:14ff.).[15] His sermon was found arresting and many of his listeners, "Jews and devout converts to Judaism" (Acts 13:43), invited the two evangelists to come back the next sabbath. This time, however, seeing the Gentiles' favorable response, the Jews turned hostile and Paul and his companion had to leave Antioch.

PAUL'S SPEECHES AT LYSTRA AND ATHENS

Of all the speeches found in The Acts two are of particular interest because they were addressed specifically to purely pagan audiences; these are found in 14:15-17 and 17:22-31. The first was given at Lystra where Paul barely prevented the citizens from sacrificing to himself and Barnabas in the belief that the two were gods. In his speech Paul makes three points: the people must turn from the false gods to the true God, the creator of the world; in the past God allowed all nations to walk in their own ways; and, God is there for all to know—he gives rain and fruitful seasons.[16] The implication may be justifiably drawn from the speech that Christians cannot claim that apart from the revelation of God in Christ there is no knowledge of God whatsoever; in other words, an appeal is made to "such knowledge of God as they might reasonably have, i.e., by 'natural revelation.' "[17]

The ideas expressed in the Lystrian speech are at the core of the speech given at Athens in which Paul "strives to demonstrate philosophically that the new Christian religion is the perfect fulfillment of the religion of reason common to all mankind."[18] Here also three points are made. First, the Greeks are "very religious." What was meant by this is debated. The Greek word[19] translated thus is capable of two senses — a good one, suggesting a meaningful religious commitment, and a bad one which would characterize the people of Athens as superstitious.[20] It seems more likely that Paul meant the word in the latter sense,[21] for the Athenians had an altar carrying the inscription, "To an unknown god." Archaeology has not uncovered an altar carrying such an inscription, but sufficient archaeological material has come to light which indicates that there was a practice of dedicating altars to unnamed gods so that no deity would feel slighted.[22] When Luke presents Paul as saying, "What therefore you worship as unknown, this I proclaim to you" (Acts 17:23), Luke seems to give the Athenian inscription a monotheistic significance which was probably not intended. It evidently suited Luke's purposes to put this interpretation upon the inscription since he contends that the evidence of God's existence is there for all to see, but in reality it does not fit the context to which the inscription belonged. Hence the words attributed to Paul here, "this I proclaim to you," cannot be used as evidence that Paul had a positive attitude to the Athenian religion; on the contrary, Paul bluntly describes it as one of ignorance.[23] Second, as in the Lystran speech, so here Paul speaks of God the creator who is revealed in the life of the nations — the life of the peoples through the historic epochs had been ordered by God. However, while Paul thus acknowledges God's involvement in the histories of the peoples, it is doubtful whether he intended to imply that God is involved in the history of their religions to the extent that God informs their religious ideas and practices. Third, God is present everywhere,[24] so there is no need to make God into an idol.[25] Here also it might be thought that Paul would have at the back of his mind the implication that the nations were all, in effect, seeking the one God of the whole earth. However, Paul does not verbalize this thought; certainly he would not have admitted that the Athenian religion enshrined ideas and insights which could be considered God-given, for elsewhere Paul refers to pagan religion as "a lie" (Rom. 1:25).

THE COUNCIL OF JERUSALEM

The last main episode to be referred to is described in Acts 15, the account of the meeting of the Council of Jerusalem.

Preaching to Gentiles, especially after the church at Antioch had adopted the policy of going to the Gentiles, was occasioning so much disquiet that some Jewish Christians came down to Antioch and insisted, "Unless you are circumcised according to the custom of Moses, you cannot be saved" (Acts 15:1). This episode must be set within the context of mission activity in the early church, the prevailing picture of which remains more or less as it was painted by Adolf von Harnack: following the Pentecost experience and the establishment of the church, preachers took to the streets proclaiming the gospel of salvation by grace, and converting the Gentiles. Then along came the so-called Judaisers who sought to persuade both the Gentile converts and those who had converted them that they were in error; for to be a Christian one should adopt customs, such as circumcision, which made the believer truly God's.

In his "A Law-observant Mission to Gentiles: The Background to Galatians"[26] Martyn has taken a close look at this traditional presentation and, drawing upon biblical as well as non-biblical sources, has cast doubt upon its accuracy. Since his conclusion has a bearing upon this study it will be necessary to set down here his main arguments: it has been fashionable to believe that in the first century there was one mission to the Gentiles, and that "that mission was loosed from observance of what any Jew would have known to be the Law."[27] There is some evidence, however, that there was not one mission. There were two missions, one of which was undertaken by "some early [Jewish] Christian preachers [who] directed their *evangelistic* message to Gentiles without surrendering observance of the Law,"[28] and this law-observant mission preceded Paul's law-free mission. Thus those Jewish Christian preachers were not merely interlopers who "dog [Paul's] trail in order to lay on his converts the requirements of the Law."[29] They believed themselves to be preaching the gospel[30] and to be liberating the Gentiles; they "are embarked on an ecumenical mission under the genuine conviction that, through the law of his Messiah, God is now reaching out for the Gentiles and thus for the whole of mankind."[31] To them, then, Christ was "the Messiah of the Law." Thus it is Paul who is reacting to their preaching rather than vice versa, for the law-observant mission was "inaugurated not many years after the death of Jesus."[32]

This, in brief, is Martyn's reconstruction, and there seem to me to be reasons why it deserves serious consideration. The main reason is that the church grew out of Judaism which had before then insisted on converts to it undergoing circumcision, among other demands. It would be expected therefore that Jewish Christians maintain such a demand if the validity of the church's origins were to be maintained (Acts 15:28-29). Again, the convening of the Jerusalem Council was evidently a matter of urgency, occasioned not by a passing theological whim but by a considered doctrine which had ancient parentage, and which had in fact been found persuasive as a gospel message. In this connection it seems most likely that the Jerusalem Council's decision was taken with the law-observant Christians looking over the shoulders of the Council members. To a certain extent the Jewish Christian lobby must have been a persuasive one, for its position was not exactly ruled out of court, as will be made clear presently.

Thus Acts 15 must have been the culmination of a debate of which Luke gives his readers little more than a vague hint. The Jewish Christian position was more persuasive than we are made to understand. In this connection Paul's letters seem to present a more realistic picture. The indications given in them of the nature of the debate concerning Gentile admission seems more clear-cut; definite battle lines had been drawn, with no quarter being given. In contrast to the picture given in his letters, the stand taken by Paul on the matter during the Jerusalem Council meeting does not seem to be as clear-cut as one would have expected. It will be recalled that the letter sent by the Council to the Gentile Christians read in part:

> For it has seemed good to the Holy Spirit and to us to lay upon you no greater burden than these necessary things: that you abstain from what has been sacrificed to idols and from blood and from what is strangled and from unchastity. (Acts 15:28-29)

This decision, strictly speaking, did not mark a victory either for the law-observant Jewish Christians or for those like Paul who had taken issue with the Jewish Christians; either party, how-ever, could derive a certain amount of satisfaction from it and for good reason.

Both The Acts and Galatians give the impression that the position of Paul was vindicated because there was no insistence on the circumcision requirement, the very issue which had led to the call for the meeting and to which Paul had objected. Thus Paul could justifiably claim that his views on the matter had been endorsed, as when in the course of the debate Peter said, without being contradicted, "We believe that we shall be saved through the grace of the Lord Jesus, just as [the Gentiles] will" (Acts 15:11). It must be presumed, therefore, that Paul did not consider the demands which the letter made of Gentile converts a deviation from what he had previously viewed as an acceptable modus vivendi. It is difficult to believe that hitherto the Gentile converts, who met with Jewish Christians in worship, were free to eat those foods and indulge in those practices which the Jews considered unacceptable; evidently there would not have been any fellowship to speak of. That there was such fellowship before the Jerusalem Council decision is indicated in The Acts (e.g., 14:1-2); for the Gentile converts to have ignored Jewish scruples would have meant disorder. In that sense, then, the decree endorsed what must have been the accepted practice anyway. As Paul himself observes in Galatians, the Jerusalem leaders "added nothing to me" (Gal. 2:6). Now if Paul found the decree to be an exoneration, it can also be said that the Jewish Chris-tians would have felt that to a certain extent the decree respected their religious scruples—the Gentiles were to be so equipped, culturally, as not to cause them too much of an offense. To be sure, the Jewish Christians would not have received the decision with bounding enthusiasm, and, indeed, the decree did not lay the ghost of the circumcision call. Later events, as Paul's letters show, brought up this issue so sharply that Paul was to feel a certain exasperation, as his language in Galatians shows. Nevertheless, it must be presumed that the decree, even if it failed to respond specifically to the circumci-sion issue, was seen to recognize the validity of the church's parentage, even if only to a limited degree.

In the final analysis, any assessment of the Jerusalem Council's decision must necessarily also involve viewing it in the light of the church's responsibilities regarding mission; the Scriptures have been and are held dear by millions all over the world. To speak of the outcome of the Jerusalem Council's discussions as a victory for Paul, and as partly satisfying the interests of the Jewish Christians, is to ignore the fact that the decree set what was a dangerous precedent in the light of our concerns in this study. Above all, that decree illustrates the unresolved doubts which the Jerusalem Council had regarding the acceptability of the non-Jews *as they were culturally*. New Testament evidence suggests that the Jerusalem decision was not an isolated instance of the determination of the Jewish Christians to dictate the terms on which the Gentiles were to be given church membership, for we learn that Gentile Christians at Pergamum were forbidden "to eat food sacrificed to idols and practice immorality" (Rev. 2:14; cf. 1 Cor. 8:7-10). The whole argument of 1 Corinthians 8:1-11:1 leads one to believe that Paul saw real wisdom in not eating meat sacrificed to idols. It may be observed, incidentally, that The Acts is silent on what Gentile converts might have thought of this imposition; if any dissatisfaction with it was expressed, we are not told. Quite possibly some objected to this requirement to adopt Jewish rules and regulations. They might very well have wondered why eating blood or what had been strangled should be considered un-Christian.

Moreover, if the evidence presented in The Acts is anything to go by, then Paul was not prepared to needlessly offend the sensitivities of the Jews; in any case, he might have appeared in this light to some of the Jewish Christians. He found it necessary to circumcise Timothy. Timothy's mother was Jewish which made him a Jew even though he had a Greek father (Acts 16:1-3).[33] It may be argued that it was expedient that Timothy should be circumcised, but expediency does not negate the fact that by so acting Paul was giving some Jewish Christians the impression that their position was a valid one, and was in fact being endorsed. It is true that at Corinth Paul was thus characterized by the Jews: "This man is persuading men to worship God contrary to the law" (Acts 18:13). When Paul got to Jerusalem at the end of his third evangelistic tour and related what had been achieved among the Gentiles, the account notes that he had by that time acquired a reputation among the Jews for teaching "all the Jews who are among the Gentile to forsake Moses, telling them not to circumcise their children or observe the customs" (Acts 21:21). While there is evidence to show that Paul was not prepared to consider the Jewish attachment to tradition as unassailable, nevertheless this charge is evidently an exaggeration, for Paul as a Jew could take a temporary vow.[34] In order to ensure his safety in Jerusalem he accepted the advice to show himself in favor of Jewish customs by acting as the sponsor of four men who were about to end their vows (Acts 21:23-24). Of course, Paul must have agreed to this suggestion because of the consequences which a refusal might have had for him; in other words, he did not act out of conviction.

The picture one forms of Paul from the above material is of someone with an uncertain attitude at best. He was a champion of the gospel for the Gentiles, but he was not above insisting that the Gentiles adopt the piety that was part of his Jewish background. He gloried in being a Jew, and yet he was aware that Christianity was not merely a branch of Judaism. He endorsed the doctrine of grace, and yet the Gentiles in Jerusalem must have wondered about him when he agreed to demonstrate a pro-Jewish attitude for the benefit of the Jews. Luke gives us no indication that the matter of Gentile admission was also approached from the point of view of the Gentiles themselves and the need to respect their cultural authenticity. This is an indication of the level of understanding prevailing in the early church regarding the issue of the Christian message in the missionary situation.

GALATIANS AND MISSION TO THE GENTILES

Paul's letter to the Galatians contains material of much interest in relation to the lifestyle to be adopted by converts to Christianity; also, Paul's attitude to pagan religion is much more explicit here than in The Acts. Paul had preached in Galatia and had led many to Christ. Though a church had been established, there was one issue which still agitated the minds of Jewish Christians and caused much unease in the Galatian church: How are the Galatian converts to be seen to be truly

Christian? Paul's passionate argument in this letter is made with this issue in mind, though the issue is taken up in other letters, as will be shown in the next chapter.

The Galatian dispute was of much concern to Paul, for he had no reason to believe that the Galatians had not really understood what he had taught them in his preaching. Hence he is at pains to underline their Christian experience. The converts had had to make a far-reaching decision because, having no background in Judaism, they had come from a state where they were "in bondage to beings that by nature are not gods" (Gal. 4:8). In fact, they were so taken up with the gospel that they were prepared to make sacrifices for Paul's sake (Gal. 4:15).[35] Converts such as these would hardly have been expected by Paul to give cause for concern with respect to their Christian convictions, and that is why, judging by the strong language he uses, he finds the change that had come about hard to accept. What had happened?

There are indications in this letter that some Jewish Christians (perhaps among them those so-called Judaisers who had followed Paul to Antioch [Acts 15:1]) had gone to Galatia after the church there had been established in order to make their appeal, perhaps not for the first time, for adherence to Jewish traditions. These Jewish Christians are only alluded to; no specific classification is attached to them. Thus Paul speaks of "some who trouble you" (Gal. 1:7), who want to pervert the gospel, and refers to those who are "preaching to you a gospel contrary to that which you received" (Gal. 1:9). More specifically, Paul refers to "certain men ... from James" whose presence made Cephas desist from eating with the Gentiles, "fearing the circumcision party" (Gal. 2:11-12). It would appear, then, that there were some Jews who felt strongly enough about the developments taking place in the church with respect to Gentile admission to want to make the point, once again, that it was necessary for the Gentile converts to keep certain Jewish laws, such as the law of circumcision (Gal. 5:11). In this connection the reference to Abraham is of interest (Gal. 3:6-9). Quite possibly the Jewish Christians had already appealed to Abraham in their discussion with the Gentile Christians in order to give scriptural backing to their assertion that circumcision was necessary. Paul points out that Abraham "believed God, and it was reckoned to him as righteousness" (Gal. 3:6). As Paul makes clear, he himself was born a Jew, but he had not found justification through the law (Gal. 2:15-21). It may be observed here that whether or not the Jewish Christians in question were those who had earlier gone to Antioch, they were undoubtedly operating on the basis of the belief that their position enjoyed powerful support in the church. After all, it had received endorsement of a sort at the Jerusalem Council meeting; the council's decision must have given the crusaders greater motivation.

This was not the only difficulty with which Paul had to contend; apparently, also, there was a question as to the "official" attitude toward his preaching.

The issue of the relations between Paul and the other apostles is an interesting one. The New Testament does not seem to speak with one voice on the matter; there is a difference between The Acts of the Apostles and what we learn from Paul's own writings. Luke presents the apostles as being of one mind. To be sure, not all of them were initially easy in their minds about the Gentile mission, and some in fact took Peter to task for baptizing Cornelius and his household, but when Peter explained his experiences they were satisfied. Later, at the Jerusalem meeting of the church's leadership, an apparently unanimous decision was taken regarding the Gentile mission. Through these and other episodes Luke shows that the apostles were of one mind in the matter of taking the gospel message to the Gentiles, and generally with respect to the church's practices.[36] Against this picture of harmony and near-uniformity, Paul insists that he held a special position among the apostles because of the distinctiveness of his call and message. As he writes to the Galatian Christians:

> For I would have you know, brethren, that the gospel which was preached by me is not man's gospel. For I did not receive it from man, nor was I taught it, but it came through a revelation of Jesus Christ. (Gal. 1:11-12)

In these words one senses Paul's determination to distance himself from those who might want to suggest that he had no more authority than the other apostles. As far as the issue of message is concerned, it is beyond doubt that some tension prevailed between Paul and the other leaders of the church. It is true that Paul refers to the Jerusalem leaders, those "reputed to be pillars," as having agreed with him regarding the Gentile mission; but this reference serves, paradoxically, to underline the difference of approach noted in the Letter to the Galatians—*they* went to the circumcised. While Paul suggests by the use of *koinonia* (Gal. 2:9) that he and the "pillars" had much in common, the fact remains that he chided Peter for vacillating, and finally succumbing, to the "circumcision party" viewpoint.

Thus it is clear enough that there were conflicts and rivalries in the church; the question is to what these might be traced. It is not easy to determine their causes, for there is no direct explanation in the New Testament books; in fact there could have been a variety of causes. One thing seems certain, however: the fact of the church going outside its Jewish matrix to find a place among the Gentile peoples must have been a powerful contributory factor.

There are clear indications that the Pauline churches were all made up preponderantly, if not entirely, of Gentile converts. In The Acts we are told that though Paul preached to both Jews and Gentiles (Acts 14:27; 15:12), he saw the mission to the Jews, at least initially, as being of primary importance. Thus he speaks of the gospel as "the power of God for salvation to every one who has faith, to the Jew first and also to the Greek" (Rom. 1:16). However, Paul's expectations with regard to the Jews were not realized, for they reacted to his preaching with unbelief (Acts 13:14f.; 17:5, etc.). As Munch has pointed out, it is not reasonable to argue for a Jewish component of the new Pauline churches simply on the grounds that in his letters to them Paul deals with Jewish matters.[37] The Letter to the Galatians, for example, takes up some distinctively Jewish questions, and the reason probably is, as already suggested, that those questions had already become part of the thinking of the Gentile converts as a consequence of the preaching of the so-called Judaisers. The New Testament material argues, at least, for the Pauline churches being preponderantly Gentile.

PAUL'S ATTITUDE TOWARD CIRCUMCISION

The reason why the Jews were not convinced by Paul's preaching would seem to be uncertainty that he was giving sufficient attention to Jewish traditions, particularly circumcision about which he had seemed quite openminded. Paul seemed to be unwilling to enforce a tradition which most Jews considered unavoidable. Thus he writes to the Galatians: "Now I, Paul, say to you that if you receive circumcision, Christ will be of no advantage to you" (Gal. 5:2); indeed, "it is those who want to make a good showing in the flesh that would compel you to be circumcised" (Gal. 6:12). The use of "flesh" here is significant. The word refers to "the sphere of societal relationships in which a man is compared with his fellow men, and the emphasis rests particularly upon religious attainments and their appeal to human pride."[38] Thus Paul is taking a stand against those fellow Jews who were inclined to believe that Christians should be distinguishable as such by external means such as circumcision.

It would hardly have been necessary for Paul to take this stand unless circumcision had become an important issue in relation to the churches he had founded. It had certainly become an issue in the church at Corinth, to which Paul wrote:

> Was any one at the time of his call already circumcised? Let him not seek to remove the mark of circumcision. Was any one at the time of his call uncircumcised? Let him not seek circumcision. (1 Cor. 7:18)

The first part of this verse, which could only apply to Jews, is almost certainly a hypothetical example, even though it had been known, in the time of the Syrian king Antiochus Epiphanes,[39] for some Jews to submit to surgery to conceal the fact of their having been circumcised. Paul is addressing converts who, being once "heathen, . . . were led astray to dumb idols" (1 Cor. 12:2), and who were inclined to think that circumcision would cement their status as God's people. Paul rejects this kind of thinking outright. When he writes, "For neither circumcision counts for anything nor uncircumcision, but keeping the commandments of God" (1 Cor. 7:19), he is insisting that the permanent aspect of the law is not the ceremonial—it is the ethical.

Paul's position, as far as these references are concerned, is in line with that adopted by the Jerusalem Council which had not demanded that Gentile converts undergo the rite of circumcision. However, it can be understood why the issue of circumcision refused to die: the Council had made *some* demands on Gentile converts, and which demand would better represent the tradition from which Christianity had come than circumcision! Thus the persistent raising of the question of circumcision could be traced, even if indirectly, to that decision by the Jerusalem Council to which Paul had acquiesced.

One may wonder, incidentally, whether in his account of the church Luke has not deliberately toned down the circumcision debate. After all, Luke-Acts, as it is generally believed, was written close to the end of the first century C.E., some thirty years or so later than Paul's letters which are generally considered the earliest of the New Testament books. Luke must have been aware of the debate regarding circumcision when he was writing his two-volume work; it must be presumed that he did not give it as high a profile as Paul does in his letters because it did not belong there. It has been suggested that Luke suppressed it in order to create a picture of harmony, but there is no reason why this should be considered a likely explanation as Luke does inform his readers that Paul circumcised Timothy and continued to observe Jewish customs on certain occasions.

The real reason why Luke's book and Paul's letters present different pictures is that they do not deal with the same circumstances. They represent two different, albeit related, realities. Luke gives an account of the breaking away of the church from Judaism and the implications of that break-away, mainly the antagonism of the Jews and the inexorable march of the church into Gentile areas. Paul, on the other hand, writes to Gentile converts who, given the insistence of Jewish Christians—and there were Jews in every important Mediterranean city (Acts 15:21)—were uncertain, despite the Jerusalem Council's decree, regarding the place of Jewish customs in Christianity. The church had asserted its independence from Judaism, but the Jews would not let the church forget that Judaism was the matrix in which the church had been nurtured. In his letters, then, Paul focuses on one segment of the church—the mission-founded, largely Gentile congregations, and their governance, while Luke, on the other hand, paints a broad picture of the church as it takes halting, yet determined, steps on its emergence from the womb of Judaism. It might be added that Luke's refusal to turn the searchlight on a debate of which he must have been aware illustrates his integrity as a writer; having selected his theme he did not encumber it with material which did not belong.

One comes back to the realization that the determined push into Gentile territory was beginning to raise questions of authority, methods of evangelism, and expectations. The church in Jerusalem might not have initially expressed its feelings against the Gentile mission; it had in fact encouraged it, believing it to be an inevitable consequence of the church's coming into being. However, now that the mission was in progress and much success was being achieved, with new congregations of Gentile Christians, questions arose about whether proper safeguards had been adopted. In this we have a familiar pattern, as the history of modern missions shows. The pronouncements made by church boards, mission societies, and related organizations in connection with mission—the need for it and the procedures to be adopted—were often impeccable and could have provided a meaningful basis for a realistic theology of mission. However, those pronouncements often came to nothing, for when converts had been made and new congregations came into being, a new set of questions arose: how could the church ensure that the traditions in which the evangelists stood would be maintained? Issues of this nature will be commented upon in the next chapter.

ATTITUDES TOWARD PAGAN PRACTICES

Meanwhile, there is another element of interest in the Letter to the Galatians:

Formerly, when you did not know God, you were in bondage to beings that by nature are not gods; but now that you have come to know God, or rather to be known by

God, how can you turn back again to the weak and beggarly elemental spirits, whose slaves you want to be once
more? You observe days, and months, and seasons, and
years! I am afraid I have labored over you in vain. (Gal.
4:8-11)

Very briefly, this passage is usually interpreted as follows. The
converts were once pagans, worshiping gods; on becoming Christians they have put this behind them. Now, however, the Galatian Christians are being urged by some conservative Jewish
Christians to keep the observances associated with Judaism, a
course of action that the Galatians have adopted. With this
interpretation, then, v. 10 is a reference to Jewish festivals.[40]
Paul's concern, therefore, according to this interpretation, was
to remind the Galatians that they no longer needed to adhere
to those Jewish practices. Incidentally, this interpretation fits in
with Marcion's evaluation of this letter, for he saw it to be so
anti-Jewish that he placed it first among those letters he considered to be genuinely Pauline. I find, however, that by so interpreting the passage less than full justice is done to it. Something
more than the adoption of Jewish practices had taken place. It
is clear, as it is generally recognized, that in describing the Galatians as having been "in bondage to beings that by nature are
not gods" Paul was referring to their pagan past. He evidently
believed that pagan religion was worthless — its gods had no reality. Paul carefully underlines the pointlessness of their former
state by his choice of language. How could the Galatians have
submitted themselves to "weak and beggarly elemental spirits"
(Gal. 4:9; also 2:8, 20)? And having come away from such mean-
ingless submission to freedom in Christ, how could they go back
to that situation? We are proceeding on the reasonable assumption that Galatians 4:8 and 9 are talking about the same thing —
pagan religion and its uselessness. It is not enough to say of v.
9 that Paul "is viewing the scheme of the Judaisers, however
well-intentioned it was, to be in effect equivalent to a return to
their non-Christian past."[41] I wish now to propose another interpretation of the passage which would take us further than the
just-quoted comment by Guthrie.

    If, as is most likely, vv. 8 and 9 of chapter 4 are both speaking

about pagan religion, then it is only reasonable to suppose that
v. 10 refers, not to Jewish "days, and months, and seasons, and
years," but to pagan practices. The religious scene in Phrygia
was an exciting one. Cults of Hellenistic origin had been
embraced by many. In addition, there were the indigenous cults
which centered around Mother Cybele, the Earth Mother whose
lover, the vegetation spirit Attis, died and rose from the dead
annually, in autumn and in the spring respectively. The Earth
Mother cults, not surprisingly, were of the fertility type, orgiastic
and frenzied. These indigenous cults, it must be emphasized,
were practiced side by side with the Hellenistic cults; indeed, it
was quite fashionable for a person to be a devotee of several
cults at the same time.[42] In the light of this, it may be wondered
whether the Galatian Christians were not attempting to give a
new shape to Paul's message by combining Christ with their own
cults. Such a possibility cannot be ruled out.

So then what had happened in the Galatian church to which
Paul had devoted so much loving care? The various strands in
that church's story may be put together thus: Paul had preached
in Galatia and converts had been made, and Paul had no reason
to doubt, as he testifies in his letter to those converts, that their
conversions were not genuine. In his preaching to them he must
have used such arguments as that the pagan religion was valueless, an enslavement, in fact; they should thus turn away from
such enslavement to true freedom in Christ. His efforts were
crowned with success and a church came into being.

Then the question arose of how the converts were to be seen
to be no longer pagans, for it was one thing making a Christian
protestation and another living a demonstrably Christian life.
The issue was raised most sharply when the so-called Judaisers
insisted that the Galatian converts observe Jewish laws. Now
from the tone of Paul's letter it is evident that the Jewish Christian preachers were successful to a large extent; before long the
Galatian Christians had come under the Jewish legalistic influence and were observing laws and regulations. Of this there
seems to be no doubt. Paul's doctrinal argument in Galatians
3:1-4:31 shows that the Galatian converts came to accept the
gospel presented by the Jewish Christians. That was not all. It
would seem that following the adoption of Jewish observances

there had been a reversion to the pagan gods which they had formerly worshiped; the adoption of the legalism of Judaism had led them back to their former pagan religious practices. In other words, the reduction of the Christian faith to a set of rules and regulations to be punctiliously followed had led the converts back to those customs and practices in their traditional religion.

Thus three reactions are discernible in Galatians to the issue of mission to the Gentiles. There were the Jewish Christians who insisted that the Gentiles adopt Jewish traditions in order to be seen to be Christians. They believed that what their Jewish traditions entailed had to be embraced if the converts' Christian credentials were to be without question. That this position was likely to open the way for misunderstanding the new faith had apparently not occurred to its proponents. Then there was Paul who was right in seeing the danger posed by the policy being pushed by the Jewish Christians: that is, the Galatians might be led into thinking that salvation was by works rather than by grace. However, Paul was unable to see the traditional religion of the Galatians in any but a totally negative light. This attitude of Paul's is basically unsatisfactory if for no other reason than that it ignores the cultural particularity of the Galatians. The Galatians themselves were, it would seem, too easily taken in by the Jewish Christians, though the nature of the Phrygian religious scene must have made it easy to adopt this new faith. Moreover, they did not apparently object to Paul's criticism of their religio-cultural traditions. They underestimated the value and strength of their own traditions, and thus contributed to the unsatisfactory situation of which Paul writes with such feeling.

CONCLUSION: THE ACTS, GALATIANS, AND MISSION

In conclusion, I shall first note that The Acts of the Apostles and the Letter to the Galatians do not consider in any detailed and systematic way the issue of Christianity and non-Jewish traditions. It was recognized, of course, that the gospel should be preached to all peoples, but no serious consideration was given, at least in the initial stages, to what was to be expected of converts concerning the mode of life which befitted their new religious affiliation. The evidence available shows that it was after the Gentile mission had gotten under way that the issue came up. The conflicting and generally unsatisfactory views championed by various "parties" in the church, as briefly surveyed above, are evidence of a failure to face meaningfully the issue of continuity between the Jewish traditions and those of the peoples being evangelized.

This comment is not meant to create the impression that such a preacher as Paul did not have a message with the potential to bring down the walls that separated peoples. That Paul was convinced that the gospel had a social message is not in dispute; he would almost seem to have drawn out the social implications of the gospel in reaction to the threefold blessing given in Jewish synagogues in ancient times:

> Blessed be thou O Lord our God, . . .
> who has not made me a Gentile, . . .
> who has not made me a slave, . . .
> who has not made me a woman.[43]

With respect to the acceptability of the Gentiles it has been observed here that the two addresses given before entirely non-Jewish audiences at Lystra and Athens argue in part that God is not far from all peoples. The Gentiles may once have been separated from God, but "now in Jesus you who were far off have been brought near in the Blood of Christ" (Eph. 2:13). The barriers of hostility between the Gentiles and the Jews have been broken down, so that the Gentiles are "no longer strangers and sojourners, but you are fellow citizens with the saints and members of the household of God" (Eph. 2:19). With respect to slaves Paul makes it abundantly clear that the gospel proclaims the kind of freedom which strikes down such a distinction as between the slave and the free; "for he who was called in the Lord as a slave is a freedman of the Lord" (1 Cor. 7:22). This is a statement the significance of which Paul underlines by turning it around: "Likewise he who was free when called is a slave of Christ" (1 Cor. 7:22). It is clear that Paul's preaching had resulted in women feeling a sense of freedom and achievement; the story of the early church shows how active the women were in the church's life and worship. All this is summed up in the triumphant affirmation: "There is neither Jew nor Greek, there is neither slave nor free, there is neither male nor female; for you are all one in Christ Jesus" (Gal. 3:28).

Granted this, however, it is quite clear that the social consequences of Paul's preaching are easily overestimated, for there are indications that Paul was not in a position to draw out the *full* implications of the gospel of freedom. The focus of the church's life was the eucharistic table. Paul was conscious of this, as were the other members of the Jerusalem Council, and this is where one senses the limitations of his message. This may be illustrated by reference to the issue of women wearing veils. In response to the protests of some Corinthian Christians at the spectacle of women standing up in church to pray and prophesy with their heads uncovered he chose to ignore the fact that by baring their heads the women were asserting their sense of equality with the men in the congregation. Paul argues, instead, no doubt to the dismay of the women, that women are by nature subordinate to men. Paul's intention must have been to restore peace, but in the end he must have surprised the women by asserting, with a sense of authority, that women were to be subject to masculine authority. In this way the cutting edge of his message of freedom is blunted.

Finally, the picture one forms of pagan religion through the eyes of Paul is unsatisfactory. It is true that the New Testament as a whole shows awareness of spirit powers,[44] a fact which recalls the acknowledgment in certain strata of the Old Testament of the existence of spirit powers. However, what comes out of the New Testament is hardly an informed opinion; there is no detailed, unemotional consideration of the matter. The early church was unable to face, without arousing passions, the issue of the continuity between the Jewish and Christian traditions and other peoples' traditions.

3

Biblical and Other Influences upon Mission

It must be presumed that the attitudes surveyed in the preceding chapters have had some effect upon the thinking of the church in its modern-day missionary enterprise. That the church in the days of the apostles was influenced by the uncertain voices in the Old Testament, the church's Scriptures, can hardly be doubted; and, of course, missionaries since the eighteenth century have been inheritors not only of the Old Testament views on how God relates to the world and its peoples, but also of the actual experiences of the early church as it carried the gospel message to others. The lack of uniformity in the conception of God's relations with his creation was bound to make room for a variety—perhaps a profusion—of approaches.

To explore how these biblical attitudes relate to what has transpired in the mission field in the modern era is one aspect of the discussion undertaken in this chapter, for I propose also to consider certain ideas which relate to, and indeed grew out of, these biblical attitudes. In that respect the present chapter takes the previous two a stage further, raising issues regarding the consequences drawn from those biblical ideas in the course of the church's history.

THE OLD TESTAMENT AND MISSION

It would be useful, to begin with, to itemize the various Old Testament attitudes identified in the first chapter.

Open Attitude (O)

O1. God created all peoples; our human diversity is in accordance with God's will.

O2. Other peoples deserve to worship God, and are deserving of God's care.

O3. Other peoples' traditions can enrich the life and worship of Israel.

Exclusivist Attitude (E)

E1. Israel is God's own people; she is in a covenant relationship with God.

E2. Other peoples are excluded from any relationship with God and must be destroyed.

E3. Other peoples' traditions will surely lead Israel astray from the true faith.

This itemization of the various notions regarding other peoples may be considered too neat, perhaps, but it nevertheless fairly represents the variety of responses made to other peoples and their traditions in Old Testament times. It would be fanciful, of course, to imagine that the missionaries to Africa of the last two centuries or so first ascertained what guidance for their work could be found in the Old Testament. As a matter of fact, there is little evidence that the missionaries had a sufficiently sound understanding of the Old Testament and its possible bearing upon their task.[1] It is nevertheless necessary to ask whether those attitudes displayed in the Old Testament could give sound guidance to those engaged in the task of preaching the gospel to non-Christians. Indeed, the presence in the New Testament of attitudes discernible in the Old Testament is sufficient reason to examine the Old Testament material in the context of mission. In this connection, then, at least two questions arise: Should mission be premised upon one or the other of these two sets of attitudes listed above, or on some combination of them? And, to what extent do modern missionary attitudes agree or disagree with attitudes displayed in the Old Testament?

The very desire to speak to others about one's faith with a view to winning them over implies the recognition of our common humanity. It is based on the assumption that the other's humanity deserves respect. Accounts of missions are replete with statements of the need to save from perdition those who, created in the image of God, have "sold themselves to the devil." Thus the first implication of the open attitude, *God created all peoples; our human diversity is in accordance with God's will* (O1), is a basic assumption underlying mission. It is to be expected, then, that the opposing exclusivist implication, *Israel is God's own people; she is in a covenant relationship with God* (E1), would hardly be a motivating factor for mission. However, as seen from our earlier discussion, this conviction leads to differing conclusions. Israel's special relationship could mean her withdrawal from others as contaminating Gentiles, people unworthy of the attention of Israel's God. However, it could also imply that by being in such a close relationship with God Israel has knowledge which others would desire and from which they might benefit. Thus E1 does not necessarily represent an end to mission, though it may well affect the *approach* made to non-Christians, for the concern of the missionary might then be strictly to *save* the others. The missionary is not likely to show much interest in *appreciating the others' humanity* as God's children. The distinction being drawn here is important: an appreciation of the humanity of those being evangelized will influence the perception of one's task as an evangelist; it could temper human pride and save the evangelist from trying to play God who alone saves.

What is known of modern missions suggests that some such attitude as E1 shaped the life and work of many a missionary to Africa. The strangeness of the local scene, the quaintness of the customs practiced, and so forth, must have reinforced for the missionary that anthropological ranging of cultures in a descending order, with the missionary's at the top of the scale. Thus the missionary's race became for its members, perhaps unconsciously rather than consciously, the favored race, the people in a special relationship with God, the new Israel charged with the responsibility of preaching the good news to others. This, not surprisingly, dictated the demand for the adoption of the missionary's Western Christian life and worship, just as Judaism had demanded circumcision, among other requirements, of proselytes.

The second implication of the open attitude (O2) is clearly assumed by the desire to bring others into a Christian fellowship. Its opposite, exclusivist implication, *Other peoples are excluded from any relationship with God and must be destroyed* (E2), would not make sense to anyone committed to presenting the gospel message to others, for it implies an end to mission. These two implications, then, are strictly opposed. They would normally be considered incompatible. However, it is important to consider the shape which has sometimes been given that expression of openness: *Other peoples deserve to worship God, and are deserving of God's care* (O2). While it may not be doubted that God cares also for those who do not have the gospel message, this thought has frequently been interpreted to imply a narrowing of the openness. Attention was drawn earlier to Isaiah's vision of the future, when all peoples would come to Jerusalem, "to the house of the God of Jacob" (Isa. 2:3). Since God's ways were revealed to Israel, it was assumed that those non-Israelite peoples drawn to "the mountain of the Lord" would be taught to worship God as Israel did. The plain sense of Isaiah's words does not allow them to be understood as suggesting that the other peoples would have the freedom to worship God in any ways they saw fit. In this connection Micah 4:1-5 seems to have been intended to ensure that there was no misunderstanding. The Isaiah and Micah passages are set out below for purposes of comparison.

Isaiah 2:2-4		Micah 4:1-5	
v. 2	It shall come to pass	v. 1	It shall come to pass
	in the latter days		in the latter days
	that the mountain of		that the mountain of
	the house of the Lord		the house of the Lord
	shall be established as the		shall be established as the
	highest of the mountains,		highest of the mountains,
	and shall be raised above		and shall be raised up above
	the hills;		the hills;
	and all the nations shall		and peoples shall flow
	flow to it,		to it,

v. 3 and many peoples shall
come, and say:
"Come, let us go up to the
mountain of the Lord,
to the house of the God
of Jacob;
that he may teach us his ways
and that we may walk
in his paths."
For out of Zion shall go
forth the law,
and the word of the Lord
from Jerusalem.

v. 4 He shall judge between
the nations,
and shall decide for
many peoples;
and they shall beat their
swords into plough-
shares,
and their spears into
pruning hooks;
nation shall not lift up
sword against nation,
neither shall they learn
war any more.

v. 2 and many nations shall
come, and say:
"Come, let us go up to the
mountain of the Lord
to the house of the God
of Jacob;
that he may teach us his ways
and that we may walk
in his paths."
For out of Zion shall go
forth the law,
and the word of the Lord
from Jerusalem.

v. 3 He shall judge between
many peoples,
and shall decide for strong
nations afar off;
and they shall beat their
swords into plough-
shares,
and their spears into
pruning hooks;
nation shall not lift up
sword against nation,
neither shall they learn
war any more;

v. 4 but they shall sit every man
under his vine and under
his fig tree,
and none shall make them
afraid;
for the mouth of the Lord
of hosts has spoken.

v. 5 For all the peoples walk
each in the name of its god,
but we will walk in the name
of the Lord our God
for ever and ever.

It is evident that the Isaiah and Micah passages have a great deal in common, and, as is well known, questions have been raised about them, and a variety of proposals put forward, regarding the relation between them: did one prophet borrow the thought (and the words) from the other, or are the two prophets indebted to a third source? Questions of this kind, however, have no bearing upon our discussion here, which is concerned with the significance of the Micah passage in relation to the Isaiah counterpart. Micah 4:1-5 reads like a bringing together of a number of oracular units apparently without much thought for a logical continuity. It may be noted that though vv. 1-2 speak of peoples (the Gentiles) coming to Jerusalem to inquire after God's ways, yet the remaining verses contain three indications of sentiments which are not quite in line with this universalism. V. 3 inserts after "nations" the phrase "afar off," as if to counter the thought of the peoples coming to Jerusalem to worship. Then v. 4, which has no counterpart in Isaiah, underlines the thought of the nations being comfortable wherever they might be. These two expressions lead up to v. 5 which sharply distinguishes between Israel and the other peoples:

> For all the peoples walk
>   each in the name of its god,
> but we will walk in the name
>   of the Lord our God
>   for ever and ever.

Micah must have had a purpose in bringing together these units here, and that purpose would seem to be both to endorse a religious universalism and to offer to the other nations, on a take-it-or-leave-it basis, the religion of Israel as the focal point of that universalism. In other words, though both Isaiah and Micah are talking about universalism, the Micah passage seems to have been designed as an expression of a certain impatience with that universalism which placed the Gentiles on equal terms with Israel. To be sure, Isaiah pictures the Gentiles as having to conform, but Micah seems anxious to remove any possible misunderstanding on that score. He is, as it were, saying that if the Gentiles thought they could join Israel on any but the latter's terms, then they were utterly wrong!

Similarly, the modern missionary has often proceeded on the basis that the peoples being evangelized deserve to worship God as long as that worship is defined or formulated by the missionary. The only alternative to trusting in one's own religious traditions is apparently to abandon them altogether and adopt the propagator's. It has often been remarked that missionaries tend to see worship in the mission field as having necessarily to conform to what pertains in the missionaries' own home churches. This attitude implies that the traditional life and thought of those being evangelized are incapable of yielding any insights which might make the young churches' worship more realistic.

This brings us to the third implication of the open attitude: *Other peoples' traditions can enrich the life and worship of Israel* (O3). It was argued earlier that Israel's traditions were enriched in interaction with those of her neighbors. This, however, is not the same as saying that there was a *conscious, programmed effort* made to adopt non-Israelite practices in order to enrich Israel's own life and thought. As far as can be ascertained, there was no such *reasoned* adoption of things Canaanite. Whatever influences came into Israel's life and thought were more likely than not to have been the outcome of an unconscious adoption. The fact is that on settling in Canaan Israel adopted the language of the Canaanites (Hebrew). With this naturally went other aspects of Canaanite culture which, admittedly, were used by and large to enhance the primacy of Yahweh, though there were many in Israel who adopted Canaanite ways for their own sake; hence the fulminations of the prophets against their people for their disloyalty to Yahweh. Thus even though Israel was influenced by the Canaanites, it is in a sense unrealistic to highlight O3 because there is nothing like a deliberate and sustained expression of it in the Old Testament. Surely the ways of the Gentiles would lead Israel astray (E3), as indeed they did, on the evidence of the prophets.

After what has been said above in connection with O3 it is hardly necessary to draw attention to the missionary's failure to encourage the development of suitable Christian worship in the young churches by using insights from traditional life and thought. The attempts which the mission-founded churches in Africa have since made to develop new patterns of worship could hardly have been made in the days when their life and worship were directed from the West.

THE NEW TESTAMENT AND MISSION

In the light of what has been said so far about Old Testament attitudes, it is evident that though the missionary could find encouragement in the Hebrew Scriptures to begin the task of preaching to others, the overall picture presented is a great deal more cautious. It is not such as to encourage innovative approaches seeing that the open and exclusivist attitudes are hardly far removed from each other.

To say that the modern missionary would find warrant in the New Testament for preaching the gospel message to others is to make an understatement. When the decision was adopted in the early church to present the good news to the Gentiles there was no looking back, despite the serious disagreements which arose regarding how this was to be done. The so-called Great Commission is as much an exemplification of Christ's concern as of the early church's perception of that concern. However, our review of some of the New Testament material shows a familiar doublemindedness, which links up with the Old Testament attitudes, and from which the modern missionary could not easily have escaped. In the New Testament we have the actual proclamation of Christ with a view to bringing people into the church; this New Testament record is likely to have exercised a more direct influence. The questions of what the propagators preached, of how the early converts lived, of what supervisory role was played by the preachers once a congregation had come into being, and so forth—whatever information relating to these issues was to be gleaned from the pages of the New Testament was likely to exercise a strong influence, and it evidently did in the period of modern missions.

Thus as far as the New Testament times are concerned, to undertake or not to undertake mission was not the issue. The issues that seemed to have loomed large were: *the missionary's message*, and *the ordering of the life of the converts*.

Undoubtedly, it is the hope of all preachers that their message will be received and seriously considered, and that in the end their audience will be won over. This means, however, that the message has to be couched so that it is understood. That sounds straightforward enough, but to ensure this the preacher, as far as it is humanly possible, must understand something of the other's cultural background. Thus the presentation of the gospel message could be such as to lead to its being misunderstood, which could result in unexpected or contrary reactions from the preacher's audience. In this connection Paul's addresses and letter, which offers valuable material for study and comment, constitute a useful background against which to discuss certain aspects of modern mission, with particular reference to Africa.

In the survey of the New Testament ideas made in the previous chapter attention was drawn to two addresses given by Paul before exclusively pagan audiences. These addresses, as already indicated, make the point that God was involved in the pre-Christian circumstances of those who are now being evangelized.

There is good reason to believe, as it is almost universally recognized, that the addresses in The Acts were composed by Luke himself by drawing upon ideas which had actually been enunciated by his principal characters, such as Paul. In the light of this one must account for the difference in outlook between those two addresses to pagan audiences—those attributed by Luke to Paul and what Paul himself writes to the Gentile converts of Galatia, with particular reference to Galatians 4:8-11. The fact is that in his Letter to the Galatians Paul adopts an attitude toward the traditional religion of the people of Galatia which contrasts sharply with the attitude implied in those two addresses in The Acts: while in the latter Paul is almost conciliatory, in the former he is uncompromisingly contemptuous.

This, we must hasten to observe, would not justify the conclusion that in The Acts Luke has attributed to Paul what is at variance with the latter's thoughts. The difference in attitude can be explained more convincingly by reference to the character of the two sets of addresses. If our interpretation of Galatians 4:8-11 is correct, then there had been a reversion to the pre-Christian religious practices as a result of the kind of preaching done by the so-called Judaisers. Their zealously partisan message which emphasised rules and regulations had led those Christian converts to go back, perhaps by an unconscious process, to the traditional Galatian life and thought which had much to do with times and seasons. For those converts the difference between the traditional system and Christianity had become obscured by the legalistic message preached by the Judaistic Christians. As suggested above, the Galatian Christians were evidently attempting to fuse together Christ and the traditional cults. This development was bound to cause Paul much pain seeing that he had wanted the Gentiles to "turn from these vain things to a living God" who "commands all men everywhere to repent." Thus the Galatians were acting contrary to Paul's advice to the Gentiles such as one finds in The Acts. Hence his stridently uncomplimentary attitude which, it may be remarked in passing, was not calculated to bring about a genuine understanding of what faith in Christ means.

Thus while in the two addresses in The Acts Paul's audience was made up of people who had not as yet evinced any interest in the gospel, in the Letter to the Galatians Paul is addressing a church of converts who now constitute a Christian congregation. While the remarks to the former are conciliatory, those to the latter are far from conciliatory.

To go further into the reasons for this difference in tone one must consider that other aspect of mission: *the ordering of the life of the new converts.*

In The Acts and the Galatian episodes we have an early illustration of a phenomenon of missions which has not been commented upon sufficiently. The initial openness which motivates mission sooner or later begins to wane, giving way to an increasingly less open attitude, especially when it comes to organizing the life of the new converts as a Christian congregation. At this point increasingly tighter rings begin to be drawn around the converts. The New Testament evidence is clear. What became a feature of mission in Africa in the modern period—shepherding converts into closely-knit Christian communities away from what were seen as dangerous influences—was already a feature of the church's outreach in Paul's time.

Undoubtedly Paul was anxious that those who had become Christians should be constantly watched and protected so as to ensure that they continued to remain such, and this meant giving them a body of rules and regulations to observe. The communal life of the converts was to be organized in terms of what the missionary considered the Christian life to be. Several passages in Paul's letters are to be seen against this background. Thus:

> I wrote to you in my letter not to associate with immoral men; not at all meaning the immoral of this world, or the greedy and robbers, or idolaters, since then you would need to go out of the world. But rather I wrote to you not to associate with any one who bears the name of brother if he is guilty of immorality or greed, or is an idolater, reviler, drunkard, or robber—not even to eat with such a one. For what have I to do with judging outsiders? Is it not those inside the Church whom you are to judge? God judges those outside. "Drive out the wicked person from among you." (1 Cor. 5:9-13)

This passage from 1 Corinthians bears close study, for it is my conviction that attitudes of this kind, and displayed by such an intrepid missionary as Paul, would have been seen by the modern missionary as providing warrant for the policy of exclusion which was repeatedly carried out in the field, in Africa and elsewhere.

The passage refers to three groups of people: those Christians who scrupulously observed the church's rules; those members of the church who broke the laid-down rules considered to be binding upon all; and the rest of society who had no affiliation with the church. The Christians of the first group were to shun those of the second. The question of relations between the church and the outside world will be raised shortly; it will be sufficient to note at this point that the Christians in good standing were to be most strenuously opposed to those who committed immoral acts.

It is well known, for example, that the historic churches in Africa do not permit polygamists who become Christians, or church members who go on to take another wife, to present themselves at the Lord's table. Indeed, one of the punitive measures sometimes adopted as a way of bringing into line members who have broken church regulations is to bar them from the Lord's table. Since the days of the Western missionaries, much interest had been displayed in ensuring that church rules are scrupulously observed. It did not apparently occur to those who were in charge of the administration of the rules that a theologically sounder course of action would be to continue to love the offenders and to reason with them, rather than to turn them out of the church precipitately.

What Paul writes about the Christians and the world outside the church is equally striking. Apparently he had said something about this in an earlier letter which had been misunderstood (1 Cor. 5:9). Paul is at pains to explain here that when he cautioned against associating with those who lived loose lives he did not have the pagan world (outside the church) in mind. If indeed many of the Christians were either slaves in pagan households or employees of non-Christian businessmen, then any advice to those Christians to cut themselves off could cause some anxiety and hardship. And yet when Paul writes, "What have I to do with judging outsiders? ... God judges those outside," the impression created is that those outside the church could live as immorally as they liked; even if the Christians were not being specifically enjoined to shun them, yet by implication those pagans were not worth serious thought because they did not belong to the church. Their not being members of the congregation set them aside as unworthy of the church's concern.

Of course, Paul's instructions to the Corinthian church must be put into the context of the time. Corinth was a problem city, known for its sexual immorality, among other evils, and it had not taken the church there long to become a problem church, displaying not only such evils as the society was known for, but also strong factionalism and spiritual elitism that threatened the church's very being. Thus Paul was concerned to ensure that the threatening forces of disintegration were removed. The question would be legitimate, nevertheless: did he adopt truly creative measures to deal with the Church's problems? It is hardly necessary to point out that such a passage as 1 Corinthians 5:9-13 must have strengthened the hand of those nineteenth-century missionaries who found it necessary, time and again, to discipline members of the young churches by exclusion from the fellowship, or who sought to prevent the converts from associating with those outside the church by restricting them to the "salems," special "safe" settlements set up away from the rest of the community to insulate them against contamination. Such measures would have seemed to the missionaries to be in line with Paul's handling of his converts — and who more worthy than Paul in the matter of providing for Gentile converts!

There is a sense in which this concern for order is understandable, for it is basically motivated by a desire for the converts' well-being; it must be presumed that the Western missionaries meant well when they instituted such stringent measures. Indeed, any identifiable group of people has to have its corporate life governed by certain principles in order to maintain and perpetuate its identity. Thus Christian preachers cannot but insist that their converts adhere to some principles of life and thought that seem to the preachers to be important for the purpose of identifying the group, but more especially in order to ensure its growth and development. It is this concern which accounts, in part, for the decision to require that converts from paganism "abstain from the pollutions of idols and from unchastity and from what is strangled and from blood." And as the Jerusalem Council said in its letter to Gentile converts, "If you keep yourselves from these, you will do well" (Acts 15:29).

However, there are several reasons why great caution must be exercised in prescribing in detail what is held to be the acceptable Christian life. First, if Paul's own experiences are anything to go by, *the possibility is very real that despair will set in because of the human inability to do always what is expected*. Paul testifies:

> So I find it to be a law that when I want to do right, evil lies close at hand. For I delight in the law of God, in my inmost self, but I see in my members another law at war with the law of my mind and making me captive to the law of sin which dwells in my members. Wretched man that I am! Who will deliver me from this body of death? (Rom. 7:21-24)

The sheer weight of the rules of life could result in a lowered sense of urgency on the part of those who are expected to be observant. One gets the impression that Paul's dogged detailing in 1 Corinthians of what he considered to be Christian living was, at least in part, a consequence of his experiences with the Galatians' inability to live as directed. The second reason is closely related to the one just mentioned: *The human inability to fall in line could result in salvation being seen as pertaining to the future.* Having to deal with a multitude of rules of life engenders a too-general consciousness of sin, which could result in the feeling that human salvation, far from being attainable in the present, is a process which can only be completed in another world. Not only would this contradict Paul's own conviction that salvation can be a present reality, but it could also lead to an even more lax attitude to morality.

Thirdly, the institution of rules and regulations, necessary as these might be, nevertheless has to be carefully watched because *rules have a way of multiplying themselves.* I have elsewhere drawn attention to a sect which came into being in the 1860s in the Gold Coast (now Ghana). Calling itself the "Methodist Society," its members, who had belonged to the Methodist church, separated themselves on the grounds that the rules which the church itself had instituted were not being adequately enforced. The sect soon developed its own rules and beliefs which did not have any demonstrably significant Christian basis.[2] The members of the church had had their Christian nurturing in a church with much interest in rules and regulations which had to be adhered to; to them, then, obeying rules had become part of their understanding of what the Christian life was all about. Thus, not surprisingly, their dissatisfaction with the Methodist church could only be eliminated by the institution of more rules, this time of their own making!

That rules have a way of begetting more rules may be illustrated further by reference, once again, to 1 Corinthians. It is recognized that Paul must have written several letters to the Corinthian church, perhaps as many as seven, as some have argued.[3] What seems certain is that Paul's words must have been, on at least one occasion but more probably on several occasions, in response to queries addressed to him by the church. The Corinthian church had come to look up to him as the church's founder, relying on him for guidance. Thus a delegation went from Corinth to Paul to inform him that the Corinthian church was disunited (1 Cor. 1:11-12). It is probable that the other matters with which Paul deals in much of 1 Corinthians, such as incest (5:1-5), fornication (6:12-20), and so forth, were brought to his attention by that or some other delegation. Moreover, a letter or letters went to Paul seeking guidance on such matters as marriage and divorce (chapter 7), the eating of idol meat (chapter 8), the value of different spiritual gifts (chapters 12-14), and belief in the resurrection (chapter 15). The sequence of events could have been more or less as follows: Paul preaches and makes converts whom he gathers into a church; in his absence he hears of some strange goings-on, from information supplied either in a letter or by a delegation; in response Paul writes the congregation a letter giving detailed instructions on a number of things; the church, finding that certain other situations had not been covered in Paul's letter, sends another delegation or writes again for further instructions; Paul obliges; subsequent letters or delegations led to further guidance being given. The rules and regulations simply multipled.

This leads to yet another reason why a preoccupation with rules can be counterproductive: *Rules have a way of assuming such importance as to draw attention away from the essentials of the faith*. The reference made above to the "Methodist Society" shows that members of that sect had failed to see the essence of the gospel. Apparently a rather similar understanding of the gospel message prevailed in Corinth. Considering the wide range of rules and regulations which the Corinthian Christians were expected to observe, it is hardly surprising that Paul's letters speak of a certain misunderstanding regarding the Christian faith. Thus the comments made in 1 Corinthians 14 suggest that there was a tendency in the church at Corinth to look upon *glossolalia* as the most essential gauge of the Christian's commitment to Christ and his church; speaking in tongues had been lifted to the level of *the* test of one's faith. It was for good reason that Paul drew the Corinthian Christians' attention to faith, hope, and love which some had replaced with speaking in tongues. Again, could the misuse of the Lord's Supper have resulted from the Christians' attention being directed away from the faith by rules and regulations (1 Cor. 11:17)?

The slightest acquaintance with the story of missions in Africa shows, as already indicated, the extent of the role which rules played in the life of the church, and this leads to the fifth reason why excessive regulation can bring about more stress than peace: *Such regulation often arises from, or is encouraged by, a feeling of superiority.* In other words, excessive emphasis on rules and regulations tends to arise from the initiator's conviction that the other party is not capable of being sustained in their new faith unless closely supervised and directed, there being nothing in their background, apparently, that could be an aid. Apparently the initiator of the mission is convinced that, given the other party's life and thought as seen from the initiator's point of view, strict controls must be instituted in order to prevent them from backsliding.

This takes us back to the subject of the attitude to be adopted by the propagator of the gospel toward the local life and thought, a subject which has wide ramifications. The next chapter will show that in recent decades Christian attitudes to other peoples' life and thought have been more accommodating, even though by and large the old censorious attitude has not been entirely eliminated; thus at this point I shall make a brief comment of a general nature.

Paul's strictures upon the traditional religion of the Galatians show that he drew a sharp distinction between the Christian faith built around God in Christ, and the Galatian religion of "beings that by nature are not gods." If Paul had written in our time he might very well have contrasted his *monotheistic* faith with the *polytheistic* religion of the people of Galatia. This is essentially the distinction he draws when he speaks of the "elemental spirits of the universe" (Col. 2:8; also v. 20; cf. Gal. 4:9) in contrast to God in Christ. He would have had no difficulty identifying with those who have pressed the distinction between religions on this basis. While it must be allowed that a religion which insists on the worship of one God is not compatible with one which recognizes a number of divinities, yet to draw a sharp distinction, to the extent that the latter kind of religion is considered to be a valueless system of belief and practices, amounts to a diminution of the concept of God who, surely, is involved in the life of all peoples.

The distinction implied in Paul's Letter to the Galatians, which has been more or less the standard distinction in the era of modern missions, assumed an even more intractable nature when Christianity was identified with Western culture. The consequence of this identification, to which I shall return later in this chapter, is too well known to be discussed in detail here. It will suffice to observe that what the Western missionary held dear was not in any way compromised.

There is a sixth, and perhaps a more obvious, reason why excessive regulation may not achieve the desired goal. I shall simply mention it here without discussion since I will refer to it again later, and it is this: *The thought might grow that one can be saved by following rules and regulations.*

To sum up the discussion so far, as the church hardens into an organization it develops a wide range of rules designed to protect its members from offending both fellow Christians and the rest of society. That this happened in New Testament times, and that the story of modern missions in Africa witnesses to the same kind of development, is a demonstrable fact. The open and exclusivist attitude seem to have kept pace with each other.

THE REFORMATION'S EFFECT ON MODERN MISSIONS

So far attention has been focused on the biblical attitudes toward other peoples, and how such attitudes might have helped shape mission attitudes in the modern era. But to go from biblical attitudes to modern missions is to hurdle over the Reformation, of which tradition Protestant missionaries were inheritors. Hence it is necessary to try briefly to discover the nature of the Reformation tradition and the effect it might have had on modern missions. My intention in looking at certain Reformation ideas is also to see how they arise from, or are related to, the biblical attitudes previously analyzed.

To take up the Reformation tradition it is necessary to recall that Paul, whose ideas exercised a great deal of influence among the Reformers, did not consider that his converts would *deserve* salvation by living the kind of life he had outlined in his letters, for as he says in his Letter to the Romans, "no human being will be justified in [God's] sight by works of the law, since through the law comes knowledge of sin" (Rom. 3:20; also 5:1-2, 9:31-32, 10:2-4; and Gal. 2:16 and 3:11-12). However, it is one thing to acknowledge Paul's own thinking behind the instructions which he issued to the Gentile converts, and another to conclude that the same understanding would have governed Gentile adherence to those instructions. As already indicated, the vehemence with which Paul sometimes pressed his arguments could be accounted for, at least in part, by the fact that the real purpose of his instructions in Christian living had been misunderstood. In any case, Paul's concern was to ensure that the believers understood that the lifestyle he was recommending, necessary as it was, would not buy them salvation.

The insistence on salvation not being achievable by works takes us to that crucial era of Christian life and thought—the Reformation of the sixteenth century—when Paul's teaching was given a sharper focus. But first, it will be necessary to give something of the wider background to which Reformation thought belongs.

A casual reading of the Old Testament reveals the concept that God is immeasurably "other" than humans and nature, and especially the things in nature which are held by others to be gods; this falls within the strong exclusivist strain in the Old Testament. In this incommensurability of God we see the seeds of the desacralization of the natural and political order. Thus with respect to nature, though God was sometimes believed to be revealed in and through nature, yet by and large God was conceived of as being above nature and nature was considered to be devoid of any inherent spiritual power. This is unlike the Canaanite conception which held that the land was infused with divinity.[4] The Old Testament does closely associate the land of Canaan with God; hence, "you shall not defile your land which the Lord your God gives you for an inheritance" (Deut. 21:23). However, the thought is of an inheritance which Israel had not in any way deserved, since God had given it as a gift in the course of divinely controlled history. It is in line with this that the political order was viewed with little enthusiasm since it was considered to be a human enterprise. There *is* a strand in the Old Testament according to which the monarchy came about with God's approval, even if this was grudging (1 Sam. 8:4-9), but the vicissitudes of the monarchy must have endorsed the disgust of the faithful Yahwists, such as Samuel, at the human pride and insensitivity which led to the request for a king. There is evidence that in at least some Israelite circles the king was considered to be Yahweh's steward, ruling over God's people on God's behalf. However many a king went against the wishes of God; hence the oft-repeated deuteronomic indictment of the kings.

With respect to the relation between God and the gods, it has already been noted that according to one Old Testament tradition the gods were considered to be nonexistent. The Sinai covenant initiated by God with the motley group of escapees from Egypt welded the people into one unit, so that their oneness no longer depended only on a common desire for freedom, but also on their adherence to Yahweh rather than to their ancestral gods. As the Decalogue pointedly states:

> I am the Lord your God, who brought you out of the land
> of Egypt, out of the house of bondage. You shall have no
> other gods before me. (Exod. 20:2-3)

God the incomparable demands the people's absolute obedience. To be sure, Israel did borrow ideas from her neighbors, but these ideas were recontextualized so that they served to underline God's incommensurability. Again, the thought was expressed that there was no human domain in which God was absent, but even that expression incorporates the thought of God's boundless sovereignty.

In light of this, the central event of the New Testament—the incarnation—serves as a contrast. The God who is radically transcendent and immeasurable has come to dwell among humanity in the person of Christ. The story of that coming seems calculated to give true meaning to the thought that every human domain is of value to God. One would have thought, then, that this would make the church, when it came into being, highly receptive to the multiplicity of the traditions and circumstances of the peoples of the world. On the contrary—and surprisingly—the church re-emphasized the distinction between the sacred heaven and the profane earth. Christianity did assimilate much of the culture of the Graeco-Roman world, but by the Middle Ages it had become clear that there were limits to the church's willingness to draw out the fullest implications of the incarnation. Medieval Christian thought went even further than that of the preceding period in drawing a sharp distinction between the world and heaven: the latter was where Truth belonged, the counterpart of Truth being Actuality which, in the words of Hegel, "is consequently God-forsaken and hence arbitrary: a few individuals are holy, not the others."[5] Again, it has been observed:

> The theological system of the Middle Ages was in controlling principles as old as the Apostle Paul. He was led by his own experience to draw a sharp distinction between the fleshly man, who is essentially corrupt, and the spiritual man, who is essentially holy. ... The spiritual man does not come from the natural by a process of development and growth, but is a new creature born directly from above.[6]

Thus there seemed to be a gulf fixed between the sphere of God and that of humanity; between the two there was held to be an unbridgeable distance. The Protestant Reformation, when it burst upon the world, acknowledged the radical sovereignty of God. Luther, in particular, took this up with undiminished seriousness, showing both his indebtedness to, and departure from, some of his theological predecessors. In this connection it has been said:

> The antithesis between God and man presented by Luther, and indeed by the Apostle [Paul] himself, is stark in the extreme. On the one hand stands the Deity in his unutterable majesty and justice; on the other languishes man in his corrupt self-centeredness; his wretched nature being curved inward upon itself, he remains unable to approach the divine standards by his own pitiful observances and good works.[7]

Luther's failure to secure peace of mind and to earn forgiveness by meritorious works led him inexorably toward an understanding of salvation which differed in certain respects from Paul's. With Paul Luther believed that the only link between God and humanity was from God to humanity: God would freely bestow grace upon fallen humanity, no matter how sinful persons might be. However, Luther's teaching in this connection affirmed, even more strongly than Paul's did, the transcendence of God. While agreeing with Paul that salvation was a present possession of the believer, he went beyond Paul to affirm that it was more a matter of divine forgiveness than of human character. Paul, of course, believed in the essentiality of divine forgiveness, though to him the overriding concern was to be freed from the corruption of the flesh, so that "the ground of his salvation was moral transformation, not divine forgiveness."[8]

There is more to Luther's break with the past. He insisted that God's grace, by which God took the initiative to bridge the gap between God and humanity, was not simply a mystical reality imparted by the church through the sacraments. In the church's prevailing theology the notion was present that salvation depended upon the use a Christian made of the divine grace which God had made available in the sacraments; in this way human effort complemented divine grace. Luther would have nothing to do with this notion of human cooperation in the realization of salvation. He did speak of salvation being conditioned by faith, but lest he should be thought to be advocating a form of human merit, he made it clear that faith itself was the work of God. Thus the reconciliation which could be brought about between God and humanity did not depend in any way on what humanity did—it was entirely dependent upon God. There was no way by which the natural order could ascend to the supernatural, God being *totaliter aliter*, and the devil being the "Prince of this World."

Luther's teaching, then, which constituted a sundering apart of the sacred and the profane, as it had hardly been done before, underlies his doctrine of justification by faith as he expounded it in the third of his treatises, "The Freedom of the Christian."

There is another element in Reformation thinking which is relevant here, and which is summed up in the slogan *Sola Scriptura*. The good news of justification by faith according to which the righteousness of God is imputed to humanity as humanity's righteousness is to be found solely in Scripture. Luther's controversy with the Catholics, and then with the Protestant radicals, led him to emphasize even more strongly the authority of Scripture. This new emphasis on Scripture meant for him the rejection of the allegorical method of exegesis and the adoption of a method which emphasized the literal sense of Scripture: only one meaning of the biblical text can be the true meaning, with the implication that all other meanings are false. Given the fact that what we can know of God has been revealed in the Bible, a single, literal meaning of the text must be insisted upon, and only what is in harmony with that single, literal meaning can be asserted.

The implications of this Reformation emphasis are evident in Luther's own words and attitudes. Since there can be only one meaning of the biblical text, which has as its theme justification by faith, then there can be only one true religion. Indeed, certain expressions of the Christian faith can be as false as religious systems outside the church. Thus,

> a heavy emphasis upon Justification by Faith was bound to play havoc with the cults of the popular religion. It struck at the foundations of saint-worship, pilgrimages, formal penances, pardons, indulgences, intercessary masses, chantries and a host of other institutions, since not merely the abuses and superstitions associated with them, but even the beliefs underlying them became suspect; they seemed to be futile attempts to build up human "merit" and distractions from the creation of the new relationship between God and man.[9]

Of course, abuses in ecclesiastical administration were rife, as was immorality on the part of the clergy, and it was to be expected that such things should be condemned; indeed, by the time of the Reformation general dissatisfaction had grown in Western Europe with the way things were going in the church. However, Luther seems to have been hypersensitive about the prevailing situation because of his personal experiences as well as his attitude to Scripture as the mediator of God's demands in Christ. Furthermore, for these same reasons the religious traditions outside the church were as unacceptable as certain practices within the church; hence the severe criticisms which he leveled against his opponents, among them the Jews.[10] There was never any doubt about the strength of his convictions which, as seen above, tend toward keeping divinity and humanity strictly apart and limit God to a particular expression of the Christian faith.

Reformation theology, then, had the potential for encouraging the formulation of the kind of mission policy which would view other peoples' religious traditions as unimportant, if not dangerous. When a tradition insists that its claims have exclusive authority, the distinction between itself and other traditions is sharpened. It can hardly be doubted that Protestant theology, especially as seen in the teaching of Luther, had its effects on the church's thinking. Even such a theologian as Karl Barth, who had cause to find fault with certain of Luther's ideas, had an understanding of the world of religions which belonged to that type of thinking which set God strictly apart from the world. Barth's ideas in this regard have been stated often enough; it will be sufficient to point out the apparent ambivalence of his thinking which makes the radical distinctions he draws even more striking.

THE INFLUENCES OF MODERN EUROPEAN SCHOLARS

In the period before the Second World War Germany was a veritable beehive of Christian political discussions aimed at bringing about what was termed German Christianity. The excesses of the proponents of German Christianity, especially its anti-Semitism and its espousal of the political resurgence of Germany, struck Barth as positively evil. It is a measure of his concern that he blamed Luther, arguing that it was Luther's divorcing the kingdom of the world from the kingdom of God which had encouraged some German Christians to think that political life was not subject to God's word to us in Christ.[11] This criticism of Luther is of interest for it resulted from a shift of emphasis in Barth's own thinking. While in his earlier days Barth tended to emphasize "the otherness of God, and the impossibility of climbing up to true knowledge of him by our own efforts. . .,"[12] he had come over the years to focus attention on "the reality of God's giving himself to be known in Jesus Christ," admitting that his earlier emphasis was one-sided. He did insist, nevertheless, that

> that one-sidedness had been necessary, and that the neg-ative points he had made must not be withdrawn, nor weakened, but merely held together with the positive.[13]

It is not surprising, therefore, that even though Barth modified his earlier thoroughly uncompromising position, his theological thought has continued to be evaluated in the light of his earlier views which he had championed with such passion, and from which the conclusion is justifiably drawn that he distinguished far too sharply between God and the world of humankind's relig-ions.

One of the implications of this theological understanding—and this has a direct bearing upon this study—concerns *culture*. The Reformation emphasis, echoed by Barth, implies an un-bridgeable gap between Christianity and other systems of life and thought. It is clear that mission policy as it was implemented in Africa assumed this kind of thinking.

There were other European scholars, influential in their time, whose views are worth referring to for the bearing they have upon this study. In his writings on Christian life and thought Ernst Troeltsch shows himself to be critical of certain aspects of Reformation theology. He argues, in particular, that Luther's concentration on faith as the decisive element in religion con-stituted "an enormous simplification of doctrine."[14] Troeltsch evidently recognized that this emphasis involved cutting off religion from culture, and was critical of this possibility. It was in line with his awareness of the need for religion not to be sundered from culture that he identified Christianity with West-ern culture, to the extent that he did not consider it possible for a non-Westerner to understand the Christian faith. Troeltsch maintained that non-Western inquirers would have to leave their cultures behind in order to appreciate the Christian faith.[15]

The views of two other European scholars are of interest here. Even though Schleiermacher and Harnack did not address themselves specifically to the matter under discussion, never-theless their assessment of the relevance of the Old Testament could have had some effect on missionary strategy. The two scholars viewed the Old Testament in a rather unfavorable light. The process of establishing the meaning of the Old Testament in its own historico-religious context highlighted the alien nature of culture underlying the Old Testament in light of Western life and thought. Schleiermacher recommended that the Old Testament, being equatable with heathenism, could be printed in the Bible, but after the New Testament as a sort of appendix. Harnack suggested that the Old Testament should be deposed from canonical rank and placed at the head of the Apocrypha.[16]

The views expressed by these two scholars—and references could be made to other European theologians who had misgivings about the usefulness of the Old Testament as part of the church's Scriptures—are essentially Marcionist in character. To be sure, such Marcionist attitudes were not unknown outside Europe; some Indian Christians, for example, argued that from the point of view of Christians of Hindu origin the Old Testament could be replaced with the Upanishads and the Bhagavadgita, considering their antiquity and religious value. It will be appreciated, however, that the views of such important European scholars as Schleiermacher and Harnack were bound to reach a wide reading public. It is possible that there was some reluctance on the part of some missionaries to Africa to teach converts the Old Testament for fear that those converts, finding the Old Testament atmosphere more congenial, might not want to go on to the New Testament.[17] Considering this, it becomes clear that the European attitude to the Old Testament has a bearing upon the subject under discussion here: *African life and thought, having as little value as the Old Testament, cannot have a place in the establishment of the church in the mission field, for they would blind the converts to what was truly Christian.* It is not surprising that in the early days of missions in Africa there was little desire on the part of missionaries to translate the Old Testament into African languages since this could create the impression that the Old Testament, whose cultural background seemed so alien, so unlike Western culture, was of real value in understanding Christianity. It can hardly be doubted that the

European devaluation of the Old Testament played a part in shaping aspects of missionary activity.

DOMINANCE OF EXCLUSIVISM

I began this chapter by observing that though the Old and New Testaments exhibit a certain amount of openness to other peoples and their traditions, the exclusivist attitude is never very far away. Not surprisingly, the exclusivist attitude dominated, more or less, in the propagation of the faith, whether Judaism or Christianity. There is a long line of exclusivist influence, from the Old Testament to the New—to the so-called Judaisers who considered their traditions to be indispensable for a true understanding of the significance of Christ; to Paul who, though he believed that salvation was by grace, nevertheless adopted a considerably negative attitude to the traditional life and thought of those whom he evangelized; to the Protestant Reformation which so emphasized faith as to sunder religion from ritual and culture; to those European theologians, especially since the nineteenth century when modern missionary activity was carried out in earnest, who considered Western culture to be inseparable from the Christian faith, and to missionary policies which showed a commitment to the eradication of African culture.

Some would argue that this exclusivist attitude is a phenomenon of the past, and that no one in our time who has given the matter any thought would adopt such an attitude. In my judgment it would be a mistake to suppose that this exclusivist attitude has ceased to influence policy, for it has persisted in various forms even in those former mission churches which have for some time now assumed responsibility for their own life and growth. As long as the churches (both historic and independent) in Africa have yet to come to terms with the traditional religio-cultural situation—in this regard the independent churches seem to have done better than the historic—then it is my understanding that those churches are being essentially exclusivist. I am not suggesting, however, that for the sake of avoiding the charge of exclusivism the churches should adopt the totality of African life and thought; that would be as unacceptable as keeping African traditions at bay, as if they had nothing to contribute to Christian thought. The point which needs to be made most strongly is that there should be a serious engagement which would expose the Christian faith to African traditions in a creative way. The possibility that such an engagement will affect the received Christian expression as well as African traditions is a real one, as long as faith, and the *human* response, are inseparable. Attempts have been made over the centuries to bring about such an engagement, but no real breakthrough has been achieved, mainly due to the resilience of the church's inherited attitudes. These attitudes have ensured a distinct unease with what has been advocated by a growing number of African Christians—a faith which lives in constant interaction with traditional cultures, out of which interaction could come a new Christian view of life relevant in the circumstances of Africa.

CREEDS AND THEIR SIGNIFICANCE

That there are impediments to realizing this goal is clear from the foregoing. In this connection the significance of creeds deserves to be commented upon, even if briefly. The church in Africa, as elsewhere in the Third World, inherited creeds which arose when it was necessary for the early church to safeguard its faith from what were seen as dangerous influences. Creeds[18] are statements of faith along the lines of traditional beliefs, and in that respect they confirm the faithful in their faith, thus strengthening their corporate unity. It cannot be doubted that the church's survival in the early centuries of its existence depended to a large extent on the firmness with which it held to its faith, especially in times of persecution. However, important though creeds have been, it is a fact that in the context of our times creeds can have the effect of isolating the church from culture. This is true partly because they speak of ideas and concepts which are so alien in the African context as to be hardly understood as they were meant to be when they were formulated, and partly because—and by that very fact—they prevent faith from engaging the world outside the church. Confessional purity may have its place in keeping the flame of faith burning, but it may not ensure the kind of faith which shows awareness of the questions that arise in contemporary society. In societies where religious pluralism prevails, creeds can have the effect of sharpening distinctions, keeping religions strictly apart, thus making mutual understanding much less easy to achieve.

It is instructive, in contrast, to consider the memoranda to governments, messages to believers, and so forth, which have been issued by the Christian churches in Africa in the last two decades or so. The issues taken up in these statements are those which arise from our contemporary experiences, and the intention is to ensure justice and good order in society, these being unavoidable prerequisite conditions to the achievement of true development. Thus issues relating to education, health services, agriculture, the weak, and several others, were taken up in a memorandum submitted by the National Standing Committee of the Christian Association of Nigeria to His Excellency, Alhaji Shehu Shagari, President of the Federal Republic of Nigeria, 1979-84. In connection with the weak, for example, the memorandum observes:

> In a country in a hurry such as Nigeria, in a community of rapid economic progress and rising inflation and various types of competitions such as ours, it is always likely that the weak, the poor and the old, the young and unwanted babies will be overtaken by the stronger people in the race. We want a Nigeria where the poor have hope, the sick comfort, the weak and unknown receive justice, the oppressed get help, the stranger feels at home, and the unwanted baby welcomed either by the real parents or in a home of adoption.

This passage pinpoints some of the concerns which contemporary developments in Africa have occasioned. The inventory of social issues which are exercising the minds of many in Africa could be distressingly long. There is, for example, particularly among the younger generation in Africa, unemployment which in Zimbabwe alone affects close to a million persons. The statement hints at, without actually mentioning, violence which is increasingly becoming a fact of life in many an African country. Difficult living conditions have led a growing number of people to engage in armed robbery, and high-handed official methods of asserting authority seem to predominate. On the last-named issue a memorandum from the National Catholic Secretariat and the Christian Council of Churches in Ghana to the Armed Forces Revolutionary Council on "Revolutionary Courts" and Summary Executions (dated June 26, 1979) stated:

> We are most painfully aware of the mismanagement and corruption which have rendered our dear country nearly bankrupt. We also believe that those who are responsible for this sorry state of affairs should be severely punished, but we do not believe that the death penalty—especially after secret trials—is the only or even the most effective punishment that can be administered to those who are found to be guilty. We would like to caution that in the present situation when tempers are high, certain citizens and groups may advise the AFRC to adopt unorthodox methods and short-cuts in punishing offenders. Such reaction is only normal, but matters of life and death deserve to be handled dispassionately and not based simply on emotions.
>
> We in Ghana, as the Chairman of the AFRC himself told a BBC correspondent in an interview, are not blood-thirsty; we are a humane people and it will be a great pity if we should depart from our humane tradition of respect for human dignity and the right to a fair trial. Certainly we shall be failing in our duty as Christian leaders if at this difficult period in our country's history we did not draw attention to the need to resolve our problems peacefully or to punish offenders on the basis of acceptable norms of social behavior.

This concern had to be expressed because those Christian leaders believed that their faith necessitated this; all that happened in society had to be viewed from the standpoint of their Christian convictions. Hence the messages sent from time to time by Christian leaders to their fellow Christians, one of which, an open letter, was addressed to Christians in Botswana by the then Chairman of the Botswana Christian Council, Rev. J.T. Liphoko. In that letter, dated June 18, 1982, he wrote:

We as Christians are known to be followers of Christ and that has its own demands upon us; namely that we are expected to be Christlike in attitude and that all of us, sharing in the fellowship of Christ, should speak, act, work and pray for a Christian society. We are expected to make the influence of this Christian society felt beyond the strong walls of our man-made churches and beyond the churches' own communities. We are supposed to be involved, and to involve others to increase fruitfulness of the land, raising the level of literacy and intelligence, turning slums to homes and directing social instincts of both young and old into channels of wholesomeness and service. This we are bound to do because as we do it we bring to our communities the "blessed touch of the hand of Christ" to people who take His grace and love for granted. We are challenged as Christians to avoid and fight against "moral dullness" or selfishness that leads to sinful attitudes. Jesus taught us to "love our neighbor as ourselves." Therefore in doing so we are cautioned against not feeling hurt in one another's hurt, against not feeling guilty in one another's guilt. Let us all be reminded that we are saved in order to save others, we are released so as to become instruments of redemption, we are reconciled to God through the sacrificial death of Jesus so that we can reconcile others.

Statements such as these, whether to governments or to church members, do express much more realistically Christ's concern for the world, and sharpen the Christian's conscience in relation to situations which threaten people's dignity as human beings created by God. In this way Christianity is made into a force—as indeed it really is—for rejuvenating society, which is what creeds, such as the Nicene, are not formulated to do. Creeds do not—as indeed they are not intended to do—open a window on to the world in which the Christian lives, together with non-Christians, in a society in which inequities, deprivations, and other evils sharply raise the issue of the dignity of the person for whom Christ died. Therefore my conviction is that creeds, given their particularity in terms of the contentions which led to their formulation, can only confirm the faithful in their apprehension of God in Christ in a "neutral" sort of way. Creeds can have a place in the life of the church as long as they have to do with faith and its implications for life in any particular place, and at any particular time. They should endorse what is at the core of the Christian faith, but also of life in the wider community whose vicissitudes raise questions for the believer.

In the next chapter I will examine a particular approach to the issue of the Christian engagement with other cultures, but before that it will be useful to review briefly, as a preliminary, the questions which arise in this connection. It is a fact that religions are culturally different, and their adherents have distinctive cultural orientations. This is a fact we take for granted, but whose implications must not be taken too lightly. Thus, by its belief system and its implications for life, Christianity in Africa represents a culture different from the culture of its African adherents. Given that fact, then, the encounter between it and another religion raises questions of identity, for every religion has an exclusive character; each represents a distinctive way of looking at reality. Hence it would be expected that every religion would want to retain its distinctiveness. The main reason why discussions on the relation between Christianity and traditional religion in Africa have not progressed satisfactorily is that the adherents of Christianity by and large consider the distinctiveness of their faith to be at stake. Would it not lose its particularity by being inclusive—recognizing and making use of the ideas underlying the other religion which has its own cultural particularity?

These considerations have increasingly agitated the minds of Christians, though these matters have not been confronted with sufficient realism. Thus it is sometimes forgotten that religions have been known to retain their distinctiveness even when they have absorbed elements from other cultures. As we saw in connection with the Old Testament, the ancient Israelites made use of non-Israelite religio-cultural elements in such a way as to underline some of the religious convictions they held dear. Fortunately, there is an increasing willingness to explore the implications of the incarnation as the event in which human history became part of the history of salvation; hence the frequent calls in our time for the Christian faith to live in active interaction with traditional cultures. Out of these interactions could develop a new Christian view of life relevant in particular situations.

4

Strategy Pronouncements
and Their Significance

As argued in the previous chapters, exclusivist tendencies feature strongly in the biblical record, and subsequently in the church's understanding as enunciated by some of Europe's leading theologians of how it is to relate to the world. As suggested here, the exclusivist approach had demonstrated a considerable staying power and has assumed a variety of forms. In this chapter I intend to discuss a specific issue arising from this to which reference has already been made: the attitude to be adopted toward the life and thought of those who are being evangelized. It has previously been implied that other traditions should not be treated as if they were necessarily incompatible with Christianity, but precisely what this accommodating attitude should entail remains to be considered. It is this which I will take up here, using as a basis for discussion certain pronouncements which have been made on missionary strategy. My intention, it must be made clear, is not to discuss the issue of the relation between Christianity and other religions in any theoretical way; my intention is more practical. In line with my inquiry, and in order to contain the discussion within reasonable limits, I will concentrate on some of the pronouncements on missionary strategy made from within the Roman Catholic church, especially as found in the Second Vatican Council documents which, it must be allowed, are the most significant in terms of the boldness with which they state certain ideas on strategy. It is clear from Vatican II and other pronouncements, including some very recent ones, that the Catholic church has repeatedly wrestled with the issue of how the Christian faith relates to the life and thought of those to whom missionaries are sent. It goes without saying that the various pronouncements referred to in this chapter demonstrate much openness. A closer examination of them is necessary, however, in order to establish more precisely the nature of the contribution they make, if any, to the issue of the relation between Christianity and other traditions.

ADAPTATION

Until recently the concept of adaptation, or adaptionism, was the predominant characteristic of the approach to others in mission situations. The concept was adopted because of the realization that a totally exclusivist attitude to the traditions of those being evangelized was unacceptable. In a real sense the concept does have a positive side to it, for it shows approval, even if guarded, of the local cultures. Instead of these cultures being regarded as unworthy of being viewed together with Christianity, they receive a measure of endorsement insofar as they are seen as a means of expressing the received Christian beliefs. This, however, implies looking upon the given Christian life and thought as inviolable. The role of culture, then, is simply to express the given Christian theology in a way that would make it understandable where particular cultures prevail. Such "translation" is meant to ensure theological unity, so that Christian life and thought will be recognizable as such wherever they may be found.

It has been claimed that the concept of theological unity "reigned up until the Second Vatican Council."[1] It is not clear on what basis this judgment was made, but I find, on the basis of some of the statements to be cited here, that the concept seems to have outlasted Vatican II; in fact, adaptionism usually has this concept behind it. Thus in 1969 Pope Paul VI said at a

Pan-African meeting of Roman Catholic bishops in Kampala, Uganda:

> The expression, that is, the language and mode of manifesting this one Faith may be manifold, hence it may be original, suited to the tongue, the style, the character, the genius and the culture of the one who professes this Faith. From this point of view, a certain pluralism is not only legitimate, but desirable. An adaptation of the Christian life in the fields of pastoral, ritual, didactic and spiritual activities is not only possible, it is even favoured by the Church. The liturgical renewal is a living example of this. And in this sense you may, and you must, have an African Christianity. Indeed you possess human values and characteristic forms of culture which can rise up to perfection so as to find in Christianity, and for Christianity, a true superior fulness and prove to be capable of a richness of expression all its own, and genuinely African.[2]

It may be remarked, to begin with, that the language in a great many of the official statements on the subject under discussion here is often too vague to permit a clear expression of the ideas being enunciated. Thus it is not exactly clear what is meant here by African culture being such as to "rise up to perfection." However, the Pontiff seems to be saying that it is desirable for African Christians to adapt the faith to suit their spiritual needs; in other words, there is a given which will have to be adapted in the various fields of the church's endeavor. This adaptation policy amounts to ensuring that the faith is recognizable as such largely, but not exclusively, by what would seem to be its external manifestations. Such fields as "pastoral, ritual, didactic and spiritual activities" should be made to reflect the African cultural reality, but in such a way that they do not lose their character as practices belonging to a specific tradition, namely, Catholicism. As indicated elsewhere, this procedure can bring about positive developments and in the area of liturgy, for example, very useful developments have come about as a result of its application.[3] However, as a policy it seeks to ensure that whatever changes occur in Catholicism in Africa should not take away anything that is traditionally, and recognizably, Catholic.

Now even though adaptionism will not, by its very nature, ensure a radical theological rethinking, and has in fact been repudiated in some Catholic circles, it does imply, as already indicated, a certain openness; other cultures are not dismissed out of hand as unimportant. That other traditions deserve to be appreciated has been acknowledged in a wide variety of pronouncements, some of which I will now examine. Vatican II's Decree on the Church's Missionary Activity (*Ad Gentes*) furnishes us with a number of statements which are of interest. Thus,

> That they may be able to give witness to Christ fruitfully, let them be joined to those men by esteem and love, and acknowledge themselves to be members of the group of men among whom they live. Let them share in cultural and social life by the various exchanges and enterprises of human living, gladly and reverently laying bare the seeds of the Word which lie hidden in them.[4]

The import of this statement is clear. The lifestyle of those being evangelized must not be disparaged; on the contrary, the Christian must share fully in the cultural life of the people. This is easier said than done, however, for the strangeness of the new surroundings, natural and cultural, may make a missionary little inclined to identify with the people's lifestyle. Thus it is somewhat of an understatement when *Ad Gentes* observes that what the missionary needs in new cultural surroundings is "a noble spirit for adapting to strange customs and changing circumstances."[5] In the history of missions some missionaries have been noted for this noble spirit of adaptation; one of the best known is Matteo Ricci who undertook the study of Chinese and the Confucian classics and became expert in them. Pope John Paul II has observed, in a message for a symposium at Taipei:

> The renowned Jesuit missionary Matteo Ricci and his first companions used to say: "We have become Chinese in order to win the Chinese for Christ." But you are already Chinese and as such you are the natural evangelisers of

the great Chinese family for which you are the privileged witnesses to the Christian message. Moreover, through your own living experience you show that to accept Christ and his gospel in no way means to abandon one's own culture or to be less loyal in regard to one's own nation.[6]

Whether or not missionaries to Africa succeeded in thus identifying with the people it is not possible to say, given the nature of the evidence required for such an evaluation. In the last century Thomas Birch Freeman, one of the missionaries to the Gold Coast (now Ghana) from the Wesleyan Methodist Missionary Society in London, acquired the reputation of being fully conversant with the lifestyle of the people among whom he was working. Not only did he associate closely with them, but also he sought to better the people's lot through the provision of agricultural training facilities. It is not surprising that the people thought so well of him. However, the evidence suggests that he could not have attained to that level of involvement where he could have viewed the people's life and thought as being of value in themselves. He was able to argue for the Methodist church's acceptance of marriages contracted by the people before the advent of the missionaries as valid, thus winning the displeasure of at least one former missionary colleague who was for the church remarrying such couples. Yet, when the first Ghanaian candidate for the ministry of the Methodist church had undergone the training being given locally by the missionaries, this same Freeman wrote to the Missionary Society in London asking that the Ghanaian ordinand be sent to England "to be improved" so as to be a more credible witness among his own people.[7]

The point of this reference to Freeman is that careful evaluation is needed to identify the likes of Matteo Ricci; the history of missions may not justifiably boast of many like him. Achievements such as Ricci's were remarkable, for they could not have been easy, certainly not in the colonial period when the life of the peoples of Africa and elsewhere was ordered from the European capitals. It would have been necessary that those targets of missionary preaching be looked upon as people in their own right, with a distinctive lifestyle which had meaning for them, and with a spirituality which satisfied their longings.

IMPORTANCE OF RESPECT FOR ALL RELIGIONS

Ad Gentes states further:

Some of these men[8] are followers of one of the great religions, others remain strangers of the very notion of God, while still others expressly deny His existence, and sometimes even attack it. In order to be able to offer all of them the mystery of salvation and the life brought by God, the Church must become part of all these groups for the same motive which led Christ to bind Himself, in virtue of His Incarnation, to the definite social and cultural conditions of those human beings among whom He dwelt.[9]

Here Christ's life is cited as an example of identification; by his very incarnation God became one with humanity, and Christ did take seriously the cultural life of his people. In fact, the admonition to missionaries to become part of the local religio-cultural scene has had a place in the church's traditions for a very long time indeed. Thus in the seventh century Pope Gregory I instructed Augustine, who was then doing missionary work in England and would become the first Archbishop of Canterbury, not to destroy the pagan shrines of the people, but to use them for Christian worship. Similarly in the seventeenth century the Sacred Congregation for the Propagation of the Faith instructed the apostolic vicars of foreign missions in China not to

show any zeal, and do not for any motive try to persuade those peoples to change their rites, customs and habits *unless they are most openly opposed to religion and sacred morals.* For what can be more absurd than to transport France, Spain or Italy or any other part of Europe to China. It is not these but faith you should carry, which neither repudiates, nor injures any nation's rites and customs *provided they are not evil* but rather wishes that they remain intact.[10]

The italics are mine and will be the subject of some comments later. Meanwhile, it is sufficient to observe that statements such as this—and there is a considerable number and variety of this kind—seek to inculcate a positive attitude to the life and thought of other peoples: Christians must look upon other peoples' traditions with respect, participating in their cultural life.

However, it is one thing to associate closely with those being evangelized and with their lifestyle, appreciating the various cultural facets of life, and another thing to accept their traditional religious presuppositions. While religion and culture are not always easily separated one from the other, it is still possible, within limits, to distinguish the so-called cultural life from the religious, for the latter is made up of those ritual activities which bring the believer into contact with, and indeed into subjection to, the spirit powers.

In this connection one cannot help asking whether the kind of instructions given by Gregory I to Augustine could have been given to missionaries to, say, Africa in the modern era of mission. What is known of the story of missions in Africa indicates that missionaries would hardly have been expected to adopt this "Gregorian" approach, for the science of the study of religion, especially since the eighteenth century, had placed African religion, as a species of "primitive" religion, at one end of the scale from Christianity. Indeed, one of the oldest reactions to the issue of Christianity and other religions is that the former is to be radically distinguished from the latter which do not deserve serious consideration, being basically evil. This is undoubtedly an old-fashioned idea, and one which would not be worth bringing up here were it not for the fact that it represents an introvert approach which is not exactly dead, for it remains the basis of past and present triumphalist attitudes. Where Christianity has been closely identified with Western culture, as Troeltsch did, then the scales will have been weighted against non-Christian religions. Emil Brunner's view of the matter, according to which only the revelation/prophetic religions—Judaism, Islam, and Zoroastrianism—could be placed side by side with Christianity, belongs to this type of thinking. Similarly, literalistic attitudes toward the Scriptures[11] which preclude any interpretative relationship with the life and thought of other peoples amount to separating Christianity and other traditions very sharply indeed.

Distinctions of this kind continue to be pressed by some, and the statements of them can vary a great deal; indeed, sometimes it is not quite clear on what grounds a differentiation is being made. In this connection it is of interest to note that in the Declaration on the Relationship of the Church to Non-Christian Religions (*Nostra Aetate*) the only non-Christian religions specifically referred to are Hinduism, Buddhism, Islam, and Judaism. While it is too much to expect that the declaration would mention all non-Christian religions, it is still significant that these four in particular are named; this is in line with the interest which these four have excited in Western students of religion and philosophy. It was precisely because of this known predilection that

> Bishops from Africa, and scholars of religion like Franziskus Cardinal Koenig, Archbishop of Vienna, asked that mention be made of a number of religions in Africa, etc. It was decided, however, to keep to the traditional idea of the great religions in the world (Hinduism, Buddhism, Judaism, Christianity, Islam), giving these explicit mention and referring to all the others in this general summary.[12]

The concern of the African bishops is understandable, as African religion has traditionally excited something less than significant scholarly interest in the West. Those bishops might very well have thought—and not without justification—that without the explicit mention of African religion it might not be readily assumed by the Vatican II participants to be one of the religions in mind. Certainly African religion, if it came to mind at all, would be relegated to a much lower status as a faith in view of the use of the adjective "great" in association with the religions listed. Such qualifying words like great, major, and higher have been used fairly regularly to distinguish certain religions from others. Those religions which have extant scriptural and philosophical writings seem to be the ones deemed significant because presumably they contain more rewarding insights into the nature of our awareness of the world of spirits, of the significance of ultimate reality, and of our true destiny. I have argued elsewhere that such terms as monotheism and poly-theism belong to this way of distinguishing between religions.[13] Voltaire's conviction that "men began by knowing a single God, and that later, human weakness adopted a number of deities"[14] not only attempts to answer the question of which came first, monotheism or polytheism, but also it reflects the superior/inferior labels which seem to have become part of Christianity's heritage in viewing other religions; evolutionist thinking has arranged religions in a hierarchical order.

Distinctions of this kind which Christians have through the ages made between Christianity and other religions are surprising, particularly in view of the fact that the various religions are living in ever closer proximity than ever; but perhaps it is this very fact which has contributed toward the resilience of this attitude. To many Christians religious pluralism is a familiar expression; nevertheless, it conjures up a remote picture because they may not have come to *know* people of other religions closely. They may know *about* other religions, but they may not have shared experiences with their practitioners. In the final analysis this is what true dialogue, that much-discussed subject, is all about. Appreciating the humanity of the other person can lead to a more mature approach to that person's faith; at least, it will ensure that the door to further understanding is kept open instead of being slammed shut.

VATICAN II AND OFFICIAL CATHOLIC POLICY

Though it specifically mentioned some religions and not others, Vatican II applied itself seriously to the issue of Christianity and other religions, though this is not to say that its statements on the subject are sufficiently self-explanatory in every respect. To begin with, it is clearly acknowledged that the church exists amid a diversity of religions:

> From ancient times down to the present, there has existed among diverse peoples a certain perception of that hidden power which hovers over the course of things and over the events of human life; at times, indeed, recognition can be found of a Supreme Divinity and of a Supreme Father too.

Such a perception and such a recognition instill the lives of these peoples with a profound religious sense. Religions bound up with cultural advancement have struggled to reply to these same questions with more refined concepts and in more highly developed language.[15]

And as to the attitude of the church toward these religious traditions Vatican II's views are clear:

The Catholic Church rejects nothing which is true and holy in these religions. She looks with sincere respect upon these ways of conduct life, those rules and teachings which, though differing in many particulars from what she holds and sets forth, nevertheless often reflect a ray of that truth which enlightens all men.[16]

The two statements represent in fact what has been the official Catholic policy for a long time, brilliantly expounded by Justin Martyr and Origen of Alexandria. It is a policy which takes its cue from John's Gospel which speaks of all things being "made through him, and without him was not anything made that was made" (John 1:3), and also of "the true light that enlightens every person coming into the world" (John 1:9). That as a policy it breathes a spirit of openness is undoubtedly true, but for several reasons its effectiveness in bridging the gap between Christianity and other religions must be considered suspect. First, as a policy it dates from a time when Christianity had little contact with other religions. Of course, this does not necessarily mean that it lacks the potential for making meaningful inter-action possible, but the truth of the matter is that in our time there is more information available about the world's religions than there ever was. We know so much more about religion today that there is reason to question the value of a policy fash-ioned in circumstances which were so very different from ours. In any case—and secondly—this understanding of the relation between Christianity and other religions did not eliminate the notion that the other religions were essentially the work of the devil, which, of course, would negate any thought of accommodation. In this connection an editorial comment on the last-quoted statement from *Nostra Aetate* is of interest:

> Through the centuries ... missionaries often adopted the attitude that non-Christian religions were simply the work of Satan and the missionaries' task was to convert from error to knowledge of the truth. This Declaration marks an authoritative change in approach. Now for the first time, there is recognition of other religions as entities with which the Church can and should enter into dialogue.[17]

It is significant that the initial policy of openness, formulated at a time when there was little seminal information about other religions, should give way to the rejection of these religions; apparently the openness inherent in the policy did not prevent an unfavorable attitude gaining the upper hand. This seems to indicate that the more the church learned about other religions, the more difficult it seemed to be to associate with them. Might not the reason be that these other religions did not seem to conform in any demonstrable way to Christian teaching, which would then be in danger of being corrupted, or even denied? Here we have a third reason why the official policy must be considered deficient: it represents a concern with safeguarding the Christian faith, a concern which had given rise to such expressions of caution as are found in a number of pronouncements, such as the following:

> Those also can attain to everlasting salvation who through no fault of their own do not know the gospel of Christ or His Church, yet sincerely seek God and, moved by grace, strive by their deeds to do His will as it is known to them through the dictates of conscience. Nor does divine Providence deny the help necessary for salvation to those who, without blame on their part, have not yet arrived at an explicit knowledge of God, but who strive to live a good life, thanks to His grace.[18]

This passage reads like a negation of the *extra ecclesiam nulla salus* doctrine, for it admits that salvation can be found outside the church. However, in this and other pronouncements there are indications that much caution is meant to be exercised in adopting such a favorable attitude toward non-Christians and their religions. Thus in the *Lumen Gentium* statement just quoted there is the expression "through no fault of their own." Similarly, the Sacred Congregation for the Propagation of the Faith advocates an open attitude to other peoples' "rites, customs and habits unless they are most openly opposed to religion and good morals," or "provided they are not evil."[19] Such expressions make it abundantly clear that the attitude being urged is not meant to be one of unqualified approval; whatever relations will exist between Christianity and other religions will depend on what there is in the latter that is found to be good, and further, what is good is to be determined by the church.

From one point of view, it should not be considered exceptionable that the church desires to make an assessment based on its own ideas of what is sound. However, natural as this might be, it can still imply a fear of the faith being undermined, and such fear cannot constitute a true basis for relating to other religions, especially as there are no real indications of the parameters by which the church may determine what is good (or evil) in other religions. As a matter of fact, those pronouncements which recommend the recognition of what is good in other religions invariably contain sentiments which manage at the same time to emphasize the divide between them and Christianity. Thus Pope Pius XII's 1951 encyclical *Evangelii Praecones* (Heralds of the Gospel) states, among other things:

> The Church from the beginning down to our time has followed this wise practice: let not the Gospel on being introduced into any new land destroy or extinguish whatever its people possess that is naturally good, just or beautiful. For the Church when she calls people to a higher culture and a better way of life, under the inspiration of the Christian religion, does not act like one who recklessly cuts down and uproots a thriving forest. No, she grafts a good scion upon the wild stock that it may bear a crop of more delicious fruit.[20]

It seems to me that an exclusivist tendency lurks in the view that it is the church, represented by its missionaries in the field, which should determine what is good or otherwise in other religions. This tendency is simply another dimension of the desire to determine what converts should or should not believe or do in order that their Christian credentials might be seen to be beyond doubt. Furthermore, despite the call for identification with the peoples being evangelized in their mode of life and thought, inherent in this policy of the church first determining what is good in other religions is the thought of a superior and an inferior culture; the statement by Pope Pius XII just quoted does suggest this.

I do not mean to say that in the encounter between Christianity and another religio-cultural tradition the latter must of necessity remain untouched; for, indeed, some aspect or other of the culture will certainly have to give way—a change of some sort or other is likely to come about. The issue which is of immediate interest here is the agency of change. As already noted, the official church pronouncements envisage that the church would determine the value of the various aspects of the other culture. To this mode of thinking belongs such an expression as "evangelizing cultures and human conduct."[21] In contrast to this it has been observed:

> It is up to the people of any culture, it is their affair to judge, in the light of the gospel, what must live and what must die. It is not the affair of the missionary, except in a guiding and consultative capacity. His domain is the gospel. . . . A culture comprises many things: a way of thinking and philosophizing, a way of relating to others and of distributing and using the goods of the earth, a way of praying and relating to God, a way of structuring life and relating to it. All these things, if touched by the gospel, become the very texture and fabric of church life. They become the theology, and morality, and asceticism, and liturgy, and religious and social life of the local church. They are eminently and primarily the affair of the people of a Christianized culture. They are not the affair of the missionary. His affair is the gospel.[22]

There is a fourth reason why caution should be exercised in rating the value of what has been described here as the official Catholic policy regarding the relation between Christianity and other religions. Not only is that policy silent as to the parameters for determining what is good and beautiful in the other religions, but it does not give any specific indication of what is to be done about, or with, those good and beautiful things once these have been discerned—by whatever means. It does not indicate where this discovery leads or how these cultural assets should be used. Thus when Pope Pius XII speaks of grafting "a good scion upon the wild stock"[23] there is no clear indication thereby of the procedures that might be adopted—beyond the suggestion that Christian thought should, in some way or other, build upon those good and beautiful things. It may be taken for granted that it is not simply a matter of identifying the good things for the purpose of ensuring easier relations between the missionary and those to whom the gospel message is being preached. It has to be assumed that the policy in question implies the possibility of the good things influencing the expression of the Christian faith; if there were no such possibility, then the policy would be seriously flawed. All that it could lead to would be that the two religions, Christianity and the religion of those being evangelized, would simply become good neighbors, and nothing more than that.

In John Paul II's recent encyclical *Redemptoris Missio* issued in the beginning of 1991, there is every indication that what I have described here as the official Catholic policy remains in place. Hence, the church "transmits to them [other peoples] her own values, at the same time taking the good elements that already exist in them and renewing them from within" (52). In other words, "it is not of course a matter of missionaries renouncing their own cultural identity, but of understanding, appreciating, fostering and evangelizing the culture of the environment in which they are working" (53).

As to precisely how this renewal or evangelization of the culture is to be achieved, no sufficiently clear directives are given. What seems to be indicated is the policy of adaptation whereby the church will be "enriched with forms of expression and values in the various sectors of Christian life, such as evangelization, worship, theology and charitable works" (52). The two guidelines given to ensure the right kind of "inculturation" — "compatibility with the Gospel and communion with the universal Church" (54) — demonstrate the desire to ensure that the received faith remains demonstrably untouched. That is why "inculturation needs to be guided and encouraged" (54).

SUGGESTIONS FOR IMPROVING CHURCH POLICY

The need to go beyond the policy of recognizing what is good and beautiful in other religions has, of course, engaged the attention, not only of Catholics, but of Christians in general, especially in Africa. Three main procedures may be identified as representing the variety of suggestions which have been made in order to improve upon the policy in question. First, on the assumption that some idea, custom, or ritual in African religion is found to be good, it may then be introduced as it is into the life and thought of the church. The consideration here is not whether or not the idea or custom or ritual in question has a parallel in Christianity; what is important is that the religious element in question, being of real religious significance, would be given a place in the church's system of belief and practice — as a means of either expressing an existing Christian belief more helpfully, or introducing a new dimension of religious consciousness. This procedure seems to be the one which has been least seriously championed.

To my recollection, the African ritual of libation is one such element which has been suggested for inclusion in the church's ritual. In some African societies libation is a most important, and perhaps the most frequently performed, ritual. Its aim is to establish contact with the ancestors and to share fellowship with them. There are a number of means by which such contact may be achieved; the most frequently employed among some West African peoples is the pouring on the ground of some water or alcoholic beverage (the latter is manifestly preferred) to the accompaniment of prayers of invitation and petition.[24] As a ritual-prayer it is treasured for the sense of fellowship it fosters, thereby bringing together the living and the dead and strengthening the ties binding the living members together. It has been argued that it would make a most appropriate ritual to introduce Christian worship, much as libation often introduces worship in the traditional setting, in order to bring to the Christian a sense of the presence of the spirit world of God and God's son Jesus Christ, and the human departed. That, it has been suggested, would have the effect of making African Christian worshipers deeply conscious of the revitalization of the bonds uniting them with the First Ancestor, the custodian of all that is spiritually and physically desirable, much as libation in traditional worship "serves to remind the living of those virtues which define the morally good life."[25] Of course, the Christian church's ritual makes room for offering prayers for the dead who are thereby kept in the consciousness of the living, but it is thought that the traditional libation ritual has an impact that would make it a powerful symbol in worship in this new setting.

Intriguing as this recommendation is, it is evident that much teaching would have to be done in order to ensure that it played the role envisaged for it. It would have to be made clear that in the context of the church the libation-prayer is to be addressed to both God in Christ and the departed. It has to be realized, moreover, that there is more to the church's life and thought than what is exemplified on occasions of worship. The introduction of ritual acts such as libation, as long as these are seen as specific, individual ritual acts, without reference to a church set in varied societal circumstances, might still leave the church's theology innocent of the concerns and ideas underlying those ritual acts which might be brought to bear upon those circumstances.

The second procedure, which has its Catholic advocates in Africa, is of a different order from the one just discussed, though the two are not entirely disparate. It starts from the basis of what are considered to be demonstrable parallels between Christian life and thought and African traditions. Thus worship in both systems of belief and practice contain elements of music and prayer, initiation (naming and circumcision, in the African tradition, and in the Christian, baptism and confirmation), priesthood and the training for it, and so forth. The church's ethos, then, is to incorporate the African counterparts in order that the true significance of Christian belief may be enriched for the worshiper. Nyamiti, for example, has spoken of "those African elements which are equally found in Christianity," and "which will have to be adopted as such."[26] This procedure has resulted in much innovative music, as I have observed elsewhere.[27] Now even though this procedure, unlike the first one described above, starts from the identification of what are seen as parallels, there is something in common between the two; traditional African music may be introduced as it is, words and all, into the church's repertoire of music regardless of how novel its features might be vis-à-vis the prevailing church music. An illustration of this is the "lyric" which dates from pre-Christian times, and which has for generations played such an important role in worship in the Ghanaian Methodist Church.[28] A related way of working African music into the church's liturgy would be to modify the existing Western music in such a way as to make it reflect African musical idioms. There has been some experimentation in this regard, though it is difficult to estimate its success. When it comes to prayer, it is not always realized that African traditional prayer has already exercised its influence. I have in mind not the formal prayer of prayer books but the impromptu prayers which are often made by members of the congregation at the invitation of the officiant. Such prayers usually have the format of the traditional prayer:[29] *introduction*, which announces the identity of the worshiper, and the worshiper's claim upon God's attention; *invocation*, which involves calling upon God, honoring God, and illustrating God's greatness by reference to past experiences, especially those of ancient Israel; *petitions*, which ask blessings for the church, for the one making the prayer, and so forth; and *conclusion*, in which God is urged to answer the prayer.

Perhaps the most frequently drawn parallel, especially by West African Christians, is that between baptism and the naming ceremony. Thus a new order for baptism which would incorporate insights from the naming ceremony is distinctly possible.[30] The naming ceremony is in a most important sense an incorporation of the child into a group through the selection of a name, usually that of a departed worthy, and the expression of the hope that the child will choose the path of virtue, which would ensure the maintenance of society's well-being.

This second procedure is, of course, adaptionist, and therefore suffers from the same liabilities already discussed. This, however, is without prejudice to its usefulness, for it could make worship much more realistic for the worshipers—provided that those items considered parallel are examined first as to their significance in their respective contexts.

The third procedure, which has been recommended by a number of African Christians but actually worked out by few, starts from the identification, not of the good and beautiful things in the traditional religion, but of what is considered to be the *essence* of that religion. This, then, becomes the means of expressing the meaning of the Christian faith. One exponent of this way of relating Christianity and African life and thought is the Zaïrean Catholic theologian Vincent Mulago.[31] Mulago identifies as the fundamental focus of Bantu belief what he terms *vital union*, which links together not only members of the immediate family but also all blood relations, and which survives after death, because the living and the dead are closely bound together. Vital union, therefore, binds the human society to God on the one hand, and on the other each member of the one society of the living and the dead to the others. This being the fundamental focus of Bantu belief, wherein lies the Christian response? Mulago finds it in the two doctrines of the church and Trinity; these are seen to illustrate supremely the idea of mutual participation, the church being a sharing community and the Trinity the three-in-one Godhead.

Mulago's views are interesting. Focusing on this aspect of belief should appeal to many Africans, for communalistic structures are generally an essential part of life in African societies. However, the question arises of whether this would be universally recognized as *the* fundamental center, in the sense that everything hinges upon it. In other words, has the center been correctly identified? One suspects that Mulago's choice will be considered arguable by some. It might be wondered, for example, whether this center, as identified by Mulago, sufficiently expresses the African concern for material well-being which is articulated in prayers and at festivals, and which is such an essential aspect of the African understanding of spiritual well-being. Indeed, the question is bound to be raised regarding the advisability of weaving everything around one specific idea. Would it be wise to proceed on the basis of *a* fundamental focus which supposedly encompasses the totality of the African belief system?

These, then, are three possibilities which have received varying degrees of attention over the last decades. It will have become evident, however, that capable as these procedures are of enriching the Christian faith, they are not without their weaknesses, and this perhaps explains why the official Catholic policy has remained essentially what it is since it was first fashioned. Moreover, it needs to be realized that these procedures involve the possibility of the Christian faith acquiring rather novel features, and this could be found disconcerting.

DYNAMIC INTERACTION BETWEEN CHRISTIAN AND OTHER FAITHS

Earlier I observed that in the encounter between Christianity and another religion the latter cannot expect to remain unaffected. The truth of the matter is that, similarly, the Christian faith cannot expect to come out of the encounter unaffected. This is a possible extension of the thought inherent in the official policy under discussion, on the assumption that there is a dynamic purpose to the identification of good and beautiful things in the other religion. Many an official statement notes the consequences for the other religion in its encounter with Christianity; one hardly finds an explicit statement acknowledging the possibility of the Christian faith undergoing such transformation as cannot be simply subsumed under the heading of adaptation. Should the church's theology exclude the life and thought of those very people who form part of "all things" (John 1:3), and whose distinctive humanity is God-given? Should it not be assumed that a people's life and thought could give a distinctive shape—not merely color—to the Christian faith in that particular context? I am suggesting here that the kind of theological reflection which proceeds deductively from the tradition of the evangelist runs the risk of negating the view that a people's life and thought can have validity, the very assumption upon which official policy is based.

The inadequacies of the policy of adaptation and of the official Catholic policy towards other religions have given rise to more radical views on the subject. Thus at the Roman Synod of 1974 the African bishops expressed their strong opposition to adaptionism:

> In its stead, they adopt the theology of incarnation. The young churches of Africa and Madagascar cannot refuse to face up to this basic demand. They accept the fact of theological pluralism within the unity of faith, and consequently they must encourage, by all means, African theological research. Theology must be open to the inspiration of the people of Africa, if it is to help Christianity become incarnate in the life of the peoples of the African continent.[32]

The key words in this passage are *incarnation* and *pluralism.* Just as Christ came from God to take on our humanity and to die for us, so the Christian faith needs to be closely identified with African life and thought which define the African's humanity. Thus by "the theology of incarnation" the African bishops were advocating a more radical theologizing, such as has been advocated by the protagonists of what has come to be referred to as African theology. The reference to pluralism was an acknowledgment of the fact that, if the world's different cultural particularities are recognized, it cannot be expected that Christianity will have the same character everywhere.

In his response Pope Paul VI came down firmly on what he evidently considered to be a likely source of the fragmentation of the church's theological unity. The possibility of such a development was quite unthinkable, for he seemed to fear that the call for a theology of incarnation, instead of bringing about new theological insights and the consequent enrichment of the church, might give rise to utter confusion. The Pontiff's reaction clearly shows his unease and the reason for it. He said, *inter alia*:

> We sincerely rejoice at the increasing vitality of the particular Churches and of their ever more manifest will to assume all their proper responsibilities. At the same time

we hope that proportionate care will be taken so that, in the furthering of this essential aspect of ecclesial reality, no harm will come to the firmness of the *communio* with the other particular Churches and with the Successor of Saint Peter, to whom the Lord has entrusted the serious and enduring role—one full of love—of tending his lambs and sheep (Jn. 21, 13-17), of confirming his brethren (Lk. 22, 32), and of being the foundation and sign of the unity of the Church (Mt. 16, 18-20). . . . Thus we consider necessary a word on the need of finding a better expression of faith to correspond to the racial, social and cultural milieux. This is indeed a necessary requirement of authenticity and effectiveness of Evangelization; it would nevertheless be dangerous to speak of diversified theologies according to continents and cultures. The context of the faith is either Catholic or it is not. All of us on the other hand have received the faith of a constant tradition: Peter and Paul did not transform it to the Jewish, Greek or Roman world; but they watched vigilantly over its authenticity and over the truths of its single message presented in a diversity of languages.[33]

The main thrust of the Pontiff's reaction is that cultural theology is out of the question if it means transforming the content of the faith, thereby causing divisions within the Catholic community. What would be acceptable would be for the "single message" to be presented "in a diversity of languages," which sounds very much like the adaptation policy—the policy with which the African bishops had expressed their dissatisfaction. This illustrates the differing attitudes behind the convictions expressed by the African bishops and the Pontiff; while the bishops believed that the "unity of faith" could be maintained, the cultural theological expressions notwithstanding, the pope considered that cultural theology stood more than a fair chance of endangering this "single message." In other words, if a theology of incarnation is going to come about by a cultural route, then the possibility of the given itself being transformed by that very fact cannot be ruled out.

This difference in perception is further illustrated by the two uses of the word "authenticity" in the Pontiff's response. The second time, the word is used in the "global" sense, a reference to the unchangeable given, the "single message" which must be preserved in that form at all times and at all costs. The first use of the word, however, is particular or "sectoral," referring to such cultural adjustments as would make the message "authentic" in a particular cultural sector. To the African bishops the "sectoral" authenticity was essential for the achievement of the "global." Thus in their view authenticity meant the theological reflection which, far from being a colored version of the given theology, would represent a thorough rethinking of what faith in Christ meant in their cultural context; and, this would be a contribution to the explication of the "single message." To insist that the theological reorientation embarked upon should do "no harm ... to the firmness of the *communio* with the other particular Churches and with the Successor of Saint Peter" would in fact prevent any such reorientation from taking place. It would require the African bishops constantly looking over their shoulders, as it were, to ensure that in their quest for authenticity they did not depart from the given. That, surely, would stifle innovative thinking. The theology arrived at in those circumstances would hardly deserve to be described as authentic. Mbiti has observed in this connection:

> Freedom from theological inhibitions also means the freedom to make mistakes. The theologians of the new Christendom must be free to hatch their own heresies and theological errors, for often it is only in response to heresies and errors that sound theological orthodoxy is generated. Too much protectiveness from our mother churches and theologians will only retard our theological output.[34]

What Pope Paul VI warns against could very well turn out to be the means of enriching the church's theology as authentic "cultural" theologies challenge one another and give the "unity of faith" new breadth.

It will have become evident that the statement made by Pope Paul VI hardly suggests a movement beyond official Catholic policy, even though the policy itself, as already observed, contains the seeds of further development. The policy does attach some relevance to the traditional religions of those being evangelized and recognizes the possibilities of God's self-disclosure being made available in them. It is upon this self-disclosure that a theology of incarnation, as I understand it, would seek to build, a theology which is meant to be a revitalization of this positive element in the official policy. The call for taking other peoples' religio-cultural traditions more seriously than is suggested by the official policy involves not merely giving some recognition to the fact of God's self-disclosure in these other traditions; it also— and more importantly—utilizes positively the very genius of those traditions. Several issues arise; the one which is germane to this discussion is whether or not the other tradition is capable of being the means whereby the concept acknowledged to be central to Christianity—that of salvation—can be expressed. Will not the concept be distorted in the process? This issue will be taken up later in the chapter.

Meanwhile, the many pronouncements which have been made by Catholic representatives in recent years have raised what appears to be a difficulty which deserves a comment. In the light of the call by some, such as the African bishops, for a movement beyond the official policy, it seems to me that there is not a uniform understanding of certain key terms employed in stating the nature of the theological task. Thus in the message for the Symposium at Taipei read on his behalf Pope John Paul II spoke of " 'incarnating' the gospel message and the Church in Chinese culture,"[35] but the address as a whole does not lead one to believe that incarnating the gospel meant the kind of theological exercise that must have been intended by the African bishops when they announced their rejection of the adaptation policy. One gets the distinct impression that nothing more than adaptionism is meant by the Pontiff. Another term which seems to have gained currency in recent years is "inculturation." In that Taipei address the Pontiff remarked, "A properly inculturated liturgy becomes the visible sign and expression of the dialogue between faith and cultural traditions." That term also appears in an address given in 1987 by the same Pontiff to the bishops of Ghana who were on an *ad limina* visit to Rome:

And so with serenity and confidence and with profound openness towards the universal Church, the Bishops must carry on the task of inculturation of the gospel for the good of each people, precisely so that Christ may be communicated to every man, woman and child. In this process, cultures themselves must be uplifted, transformed and permeated by Christ's original message of divine truth, without harming what is noble in them. Hence worthy African traditions are to be preserved. Moreover, in accordance with the full truth of the gospels and in harmony with the magisterium of the Church, living and dynamic African traditions are to be consolidated.[36]

Here the official Catholic policy is echoed in the expressions "without harming what is noble in them" and "worthy African traditions are to be preserved," though, as noted earlier, statements of this kind hardly give any indication of what the identification of noble things should lead to. Furthermore, there is no suggestion here that "inculturation of the gospel" meant anything more than adapting the message to suit the local cultural needs. It evidently carries with it no hint of a more radical theological exercise than is suggested by the concept of indigenization or adaptation.

Thus the expression "a theology of incarnation/incarnating the gospel in a culture," "adaptation/translation," and "inculturation" do not seem to be readily distinguishable one from the other as to their significance. This impression is strengthened by a papal message given to bishops of Kenya who were on a visit to Rome. In that message Pope John Paul II said, among other things:

As for the life and ministry of priests and religious in your country, it is clear that they have a special role and responsibility in *"incarnating" the gospel in the culture* of the people whom they serve. The word of God is directed to all cultures, and the task is to translate the treasure of the faith, in all its originality and without betrayal, into the legitimate variety of expressions found among the various peoples of the world. Inculturation is not the simple assimilation of local customs, expressions or outlooks into the life of the Church. It proceeds above all from the very power of the gospel to transform, purify and elevate the genius and values of every culture. Once the elements of a particular culture are seen truly to conform to the revealed message as held and transmitted by the Church, then can they be incorporated into the worship, life and ministry of the ecclesial community. There is always a need for a genuine discernment that is subject to a corresponding pastoral charism entrusted to the magisterium of the bishops.[37]

If there is a statement that demonstrates most clearly the uncertainty surrounding the official Catholic policy, it is this one. To begin with, the three expressions, "incarnating the gospel" in a people's culture, "to translate the treasure of the faith," and "inculturation" seem to be understood here to be interchangeable. Furthermore, if it is assumed, as it must be, that what these expressions signify does not run counter to the official Catholic policy towards other traditions,[38] then the conclusion is unavoidable that the official attitude toward the quest for what is often referred to as African theology is bound to be negative. This quest, as previously explained, calls for a more committed engagement with African life and thought than the official policy would want to endorse. Indeed, if the official policy is on par with the concept of translation or adaptation, then it does not view traditional religio-cultural systems as partners in any but the ordinary sense.

THREE APPROACHES TO DISCOVERING A DISTINCTIVE CHRISTIANITY

What the above discussion has established so far is that there is a long-standing official Catholic policy which looks with some favor upon other traditions, and that certain terms have come into use as a means of expressing the openness inherent in that policy. These terms, however, seem to be variously understood within the Catholic community, mainly because of what appears to be a lack of precision regarding their use. Not surprisingly, therefore, in Catholicism, especially in the Third World, one finds a variety of approaches to the issue of discovering a distinctive Christianity.

It is possible to discern three main approaches, the first of which starts with seeking to rid the church's ethos of demonstrably Western elements, such as the lighting of candles and the celebration of the feasts of European saints. When we consider that the idea of eliminating Western elements arises from the reassertion of traditional culture and from the desire to avoid the charge of Catholicism being a foreign religion, then it becomes clear that what is being urged here is the desirability of enhancing the local culture. This approach, then, may amount to nothing more than adaptionism, which has been recommended by some Catholics in India, a country which can boast of such ancient Hindu scriptures as the Bhagavadgita.[39] It is hardly necessary to reiterate the point that adaptionism, in whatever form, may not lead to a distinctive Christian expression if pursued by itself.

A second approach which has over the last decades received the blessing of the Christian church in general, and which very much accords with the views expressed in Vatican II's Declaration on the Relationship of the Church to Non-Christian Religions (*Nostra Aetate*), is interfaith dialogue, the purpose of which is to identify those ideas which are held in common by Christians and non-Christians. It is not immediately clear what is to be done when such common elements are discerned, although church documents seem to regard favorably the possibility of practical collaboration which is rooted in this common ground and aimed at alleviating human suffering.

A third approach—one which may be characterized as a thoroughgoing assimilation of various elements in non-Christian religious traditions—raises the issue of what account is to be taken of indigenous religions. This is where some radical proposals which go well beyond the official Catholic policy have been advocated. In this regard the experiments going on in Catholicism in India are quite striking, though the presuppositions underlying them continue to be challenged. Thus some Indian Catholic priests have expressed the conviction that Christianity does not have exclusive validity in the world of religions;

indeed, some claim that all religions have equal validity. That being so, attempts to convert others must be seen as amounting to "spiritual selfishness." The way forward might even lie in abandoning the Bible and traditional Christian theology altogether, and instead dwelling for spiritual growth on the sacred Hindu texts. Ironically, one of the centers in India for a radical rethinking of Catholicism is the National Catechetical and Liturgical Centre which was founded by the Indian bishops in 1966, the year following the conclusion of Vatican II. Vatican II might have been seen as encouraging this experimentation, but in the light of the above analysis of some of Catholicism's pronouncements, it becomes clear that some experiments by some Indian Catholic priests go far beyond what was envisaged by Vatican II, which upholds the policy described here as official. Indeed, the Catholic church could justifiably outlaw certain theological innovations, especially those which entail the total displacement of the Bible, for this would be separating the church from its historical roots.

If the question is asked why Catholics who recommend such transformations of Christian tradition favor a more radical approach than the official Catholic policy indicates, the reason is, surely, that they consider the official policy to be inadequate, its main weakness lying in the fact that it does not involve any real engagement with the life and thought of the people being evangelized. Whatever one might say about that policy's implied openness, it is essentially exclusivist, in fact. It seems to be more an expression of the church's concern to preserve its unity on the basis of an approved statement of faith than to allow for the possibility of the "single message" making room for *statements* of faith. Evidently the advocates of the new experiments in theological thought believe that the church's interests will be best served by relaxing this exclusivist stance, in order for it not only to be seen to demonstrate the fallacy of the church fostering spiritual colonialism, but also—and more importantly—to enrich its own teaching.

Inevitably, then, the question must be raised of why the official Catholic policy has remained what it is today, long after it was first formulated. In this connection, it has already been observed that the risk of a closer engagement with other traditions resulting in the "unity" of the Catholic faith being jeopardized is seen to be a real one; to maintain church tradition is considered to be essential if Catholicism is to be prevented from becoming nominal, and thus losing its distinctiveness. Furthermore, when all is said and done, it remains a fact that the traditions of Catholicism, like those of the other historic churches, were developed and nurtured in a world which was and remains culturally different from the Third World. The cultural world of Catholicism is of course Western, and the history of Christianity, with reference to its spread in the Third World, has amply demonstrated the resilience of its Western cultural character in the face of change. When Pius XII spoke of the church calling people "to a higher culture and a better way of life" he could not have had in mind spiritual upliftment alone. The plain sense of the passage in which this statement is expressed does not allow such a partial interpretation of it, for the passage in fact contrasts "a higher culture and a better way of life" with a "wild stock," the latter representing the way of life of people in "any new land."[40] The traditional Catholic policy does ensure the preservation of the church's traditions and their Western flavor, even though attempts have been made, especially since Vatican II, to tone down this flavor with the adoption of liturgical practices such as celebrating Mass in the local languages.

A third possible reason why there appears to be no eagerness to go much further than the official policy lies surely in the fear that a closer engagement with other religio-cultural traditions would result in the central message of Christianity—salvation in Christ—becoming distorted. Indeed, that message could hardly be articulated in all its fullness should Christianity become too closely aligned with other traditions, since the latter do not have a comparable understanding of salvation. This is a large subject which cannot be treated here in any meaningful detail; it will suffice to approach it in a preliminary fashion, having in mind Christianity and African traditional religion.

SALVATION RELIGIONS

Religions are not the same; each has its own content and style of belief and practice which set it apart from the other religions. Not surprisingly, therefore, a problem arises when an attempt is made to relate Christianity and another religion – a notoriously difficult procedure since it is not easy to determine the criteria which might be used in such an exercise. There is one criterion, however, which has increasingly come under scrutiny, and that is whether or not the other religion is one of salvation.

As soon as one uses the word salvation one becomes aware of the possibility of its significance being colored by the one-sided, and yet widely held, Christian understanding of it as the unrolling of a personal sin through Christ's death on the cross. Of course, salvation does involve being made to be at peace with God through Christ's work of removing the barrier between God and us. However, to listen to the Scriptures is to be aware that salvation also involves a material, this-worldly element: peace and well-being in the context of our physical and material circumstances. One only has to recall Jesus' offer of forgiveness to the physically handicapped to be aware that Jesus understood salvation to have material consequences as well. Christian theology has not always resisted the temptation to "spiritualize" the concept of salvation to the extent of ignoring the strong biblical evidence which suggests that salvation implies the restoration of a person, or a group of persons, to wholeness, with consequences reaching beyond that individual or group.

African religion makes provision for the restoration and maintenance of wholeness. Sawyerr has identified those situations which call for ritual acts whose purpose is the restoration of equilibrium.[41] Some of these situations relate to our material vicissitudes, such as unemployment, hunger, and so forth. These play havoc with not only the individual's but also the society's well-being, which is not surprising given the proverbially delicate interrelationships which link members of a society one to the other. The need for individual-community wholeness is of vital importance to the African. Life on this earth must be such as to reinforce this wholeness; the spirit powers do not look kindly upon actions which destroy that intrasocietal harmony which ensures wholeness. This explains why, in some societies at least, not all the dead are believed to survive in the same way. Thus among the Akan of Ghana, those who did not live worthy lives are not called upon during rites in connection with the dead, and they may not have children named after them; indeed, the Lo daGaa of Ghana have a rigorous eschatology which stipulates a variety of sanctions to be applied to the dead for wrong-doing while in the world of the living.[42] It is clearly understood by African peoples, and expressed in a variety of ways, that the life which one lives here matters.

In addition to situations relating to our material circumstances, there are others which concern the infringement of ritual rules or the commission of acts which in some way or other displease the spirit powers. Of course, in a sense the displeasure of the spirit powers is an element in *all* situations from which the African seeks relief, so that to distinguish between material and "spiritual" situations may not always be a realistic procedure. Not only is life understood to be a unity, but evil situations ultimately have consequences for the individual as well as for the community as a whole.

African religion makes provision for a variety of ritual acts for the purpose of bringing relief from evil situations; sacrifices, in particular, are available to restore the right relationships on which wholeness thrives. It is here that one must raise the question of the efficacy of these ritual provisions. Of course, sacrifices are made in the belief that they are capable of getting rid of evil situations. However, questions begin to arise when one considers such ritual areas as the variety of spirit recipients of ritual attention. First, much less formal worship is given to God than to the other spirit powers; indeed, it has been observed that sacrifice to God is so infrequently made among the Ibo of eastern Nigeria that the ordinary person may not be aware of it as a viable option.[43] Secondly, sometimes sacrifices are offered, not in order to bring the spirit power closer in fellowship, but in order to repel and drive it away. This is particularly true of sacrifices intended for warding off evil, such as might be offered to baneful spirits.[44] Thirdly, there is the tendency to consider the spirit powers to be under pressure to do the wishes of the worshiper. In other words, sacrifices are often thought of as *opera operata* — when the right procedures have been gone through, the spirit powers have no option but to grant what is desired. Indeed, among some peoples, when the worshiper's desires have not been fulfilled, the option may be considered of turning to another spirit power.[45]

The point of the comments made in the preceding paragraph is that the Christian cannot but be aware of the possibility that some of the ideas underlying African beliefs and practices lead to misunderstanding of the Christian teaching on salvation. The fact remains, nevertheless, that the concept of salvation/wholeness is not alien to African religion; as a matter of fact, the African understanding could be an important corrective to the popular misrepresentation of the Christian concept which limits the significance of salvation.

There is yet another reason for the official Catholic policy having remained unchanged for so long. It is worth remembering that this doctrine is seen to have a scriptural basis, particularly in the opening verses of John's Gospel. The question then arises of the extent to which warrant might be found in the Scriptures for the more radical involvement with other traditions such as that advocated by the African bishops with their call for a theology of incarnation. As far as that is concerned, the Scriptures hardly provide a direct warrant. Whatever indications there might be of the desirability of a closer engagement with other traditions are to be found largely in the Old Testament, as my earlier chapters show. However, there is a more fundamental consideration which makes the inquiry regarding scriptural warrant largely superfluous: the concerns expressed by the African bishops relate to questions which were not in the minds of the scriptural authors. Even where, as in the Old Testament times, the understanding of God was enriched in interaction with other peoples' life and thought, such enrichment did not occur through any programmed engagement. The chances are that a deliberate and programmed engagement might have been resisted, just as Antiochus Epiphanes' decree proscribing the Jewish religion jolted the Jews into resisting their Syrian masters at a time when some Jews had already embraced Hellenism and all that it stood for.

I have not intended to create the impression that the uncertainty surrounding the issue of what attitude is to be adopted toward other traditions is peculiarly Catholic. The truth of the matter is that of the historic churches whose missionaries went out to countries in the Third World, it is the Catholic church more than any other that has repeatedly considered this issue in order to discover how best to present the gospel to others. Outside the Catholic church official pronouncements of this kind are not easy to find — certainly not in such concentration — in contemporary times. If I have been critical of the Catholic policy here, it is because, useful and forward-looking as it is, it is nevertheless essentially exclusivist. In one breath it endorses traditional religious insights and in the other it warns against far-reaching developments, thus stopping short of a committed engagement with the other religions.

5

Exclusivism and the Church Today

The previous chapter has, among other things, established the fact of the Western church's dissatisfaction with exclusivist policies. At the same time, however, it has shown that it has not been easy trying to rid the mission enterprise of all exclusivist tendencies, for the history of missions witnesses to a wide range of such tendencies. The most glaring illustration of these is the *tabula rasa* doctrine which maintains that the culture of those being evangelized cannot be looked upon in any way as a basis upon which to build; for Christianity to establish roots among the people, their culture, according to this doctrine, must give way altogether. Accompanying this doctrine is the understanding of mission as a "civilizing" process. It was David Livingstone's expectation that missionaries would help make Africans "gentlemen, civilized and Christian."[1] This, of course, has an exclusivist ring about it. It is in line with Troeltsch's conviction that it was not really possible to speak about the Christian faith to a non-European. Nevertheless, mission understood as a Westernization process was pursued with such devotion that in the early days of missions in Africa some of the most ardent supporters of the Westernization of the church were the African converts themselves, especially those who had been brought up in the mission schools. Since the mission-founded churches became independent they have by and large continued to demonstrate their attachment to the ways of the Western churches from whose efforts they had come into being.

But even in those early days of missions in Africa not everyone considered this Westernization to be a healthy process. Some missionaries questioned the wisdom of such a policy, as did others within and without the church. Thus there were those Africans outside the church who did not look with favor upon Christianity because of what they felt it could do to their culture. This was precisely what the Asantehene Mensa Bonsu said to Reverend Picot of the Wesleyan Methodist Missionary Society on the latter's visit to Kumasi, Ghana, in 1876:

> We know God already ourselves. . . . As to the commandments of God, we know that we keep them all. We keep the first through our fetishes. In Ashanti we do not allow people to abuse the name of God. As to keeping the sabbath we have always kept it. If a man steals we kill him, as the British killed a man in Kumasi for stealing. If a man takes the wife of another we kill him. If a man commits murder we kill him too. But we will never embrace your religion for it would make our people proud. It is your religion that has ruined the Fanti country, weakening their power, and brought down the high man on a level with the low man.[2]

The King of Asante expressed an unwillingness to recognize the missionary effort on the grounds of what he rightly discerned as a potential clash of cultures. As I have suggested elsewhere, it is all too easy to dismiss the disturbances which erupted time and again in the mission areas in Africa as the outcome of an irrational dislike for the foreign preachers; there seems to have been a clear understanding of the missionary preaching's potential for affecting adversely the cohesion of the local cultures.[3]

It is this culture clash, with the Western missionary's culture appearing to be the superior culture, which has led to the proposal of certain radical solutions. Two such solutions, which I wish to refer to now, have emanated from outside the church.

They share the conviction that Christianity should not be considered suitable for the African because it represents another culture altogether. The African dignity demands, therefore, that Christianity be jettisoned. In the early days of political emancipation many an African politician expressed the view that Christianity, as an arm of Western colonial power, must therefore be considered a blot upon the people's selfhood. Not much came of these outbursts, mainly because many of those early political leaders, having been brought up in mission schools themselves, thought too well of their Christian affiliation to want to destroy Christianity. For some, however, hope continues to burn that Christianity will be eclipsed in the African quest for selfhood.

MOVEMENTS IN THE AFRICAN QUEST FOR RELIGIOUS IDENTITY

One such person is the Ghanaian Osofo-Okomfo Damuah, formerly a priest of the Roman Catholic church. In recent years not only has he severed all links with the church, but he has also started a religious movement aimed at enabling Africans to worship God in a way that reflects their Africanness. This religion, named by its founder Afrikania Mission, sets out to take, in its founder's words, the "best of the past, present and future, to create a new synthesis to guide man in his quest for God and total human development."[4] Damuah is not the most coherent expositor of his own ideas and vision, but he quite clearly intends to present African traditional religion in a new light, dressed up in such a way as to make it into a faith with which the modern African will identify. Hence the importance which this Mission attaches to religion as being able to aid development goals, save people from oppression, decadence, ignorance, and so forth. Thus Afrocentricism, the term used for the African's self-knowledge and desire to work effectively for the development of the African continent, is the central concern of Afrikania Mission.

As yet Afrikania Mission does not have its own scriptures; they are in the process of being compiled. It is not possible to say now what they are going to consist of. This much seems certain, however: they are in all probability going to owe much to the *Egyptian Book of the Dead*, if the frequent references to it are anything to go by. Since the ancient Egyptians are held to be African,[5] this Egyptian book is seen as a measure of the glory of the African culture; hence the high regard in which it is held by Damuah. Afrikania Mission regards Jesus as a son of God, one of several, in fact, for such personalities of earlier days as Okomfo Anokye, the traditional priestess of Asante fame, Kwame Nkrumah, president of the First Republic of Ghana, and others are also considered "sons" of God, and they are invoked in libation prayers in worship services.

By no stretch of the imagination can Afrikania Mission be looked upon as an Africanized form of Christianity, as some had earlier thought. It is considered by its founder and leader to be more authentic in Africa than Christianity because of the attention it pays to traditional forms of spirituality. This is not the place to raise the issue of whether or not Afrikania Mission does indeed represent African traditional spirituality. I suspect that practitioners of African traditional religion will have problems identifying with it even though it makes use of such practices as libation. The Mission is in its early stages, having been inaugurated on December 22, 1983. Although branches have been established in a number of towns and villages, there is as yet no inkling of a groundswell of interest in it. One hesitates to assign a reason for this, but one does get the impression from conversations with Damuah and from the Mission's worship services that Afrikania Mission is rather contrived; it gives the impression of having been put together in a laboratory, with facets of a variety of traditions brought together to constitute it.

Afrikania Mission is only one attempt made in our time to give the African an alternative to Christianity which has strong ties with traditional Africa. In 1975 representative practitioners of African traditional religion came together from various parts of Nigeria to consider taking part in the Second World Black and African Festival of Arts and Culture (FESTAC). From this meeting there issued a declaration on the basis of which it was agreed to feature African traditional religion in the festival's activities. The declaration read in part:

Whereas for the past many centuries Europe's Christianity and Arab's Islam had been misrepresenting Black Africa's traditional religions as Paganism and deriding Black Africans as worshippers of false gods, all of us in Nigeria who still practice Africa's religious traditions, are now resolved to organise all the traditional religions of Nigeria into a united front under the coordinating philosophy of Godianism as the appropriate philosophical identification of Black Africa's traditional religious behaviors, with a view, not only to tell that Black Africans were at no hour of human history pagans, but also to show that Black Africa has a religious civilization to offer to a world which foreign religions have confused into a chaotic asylum from which religious harmony has fled.[6]

Godianism, mentioned in this excerpt, has, under its chief high priest, Chief K. O. K. Onyioha, made what appears so far to have been an unsuccessful bid to give leadership to African traditional religions in Nigeria. This, however, is not a measure of Chief Onyioha's commitment to the task of giving African religio-cultural traditions a greater visibility at the expense of Christianity.

Movements outside the church, with their implied or stated rejection of Christianity, are only one aspect of the reaction against the Westernism which was fostered by missionaries, and which largely remains in place in the historic churches in Africa and elsewhere in the Third World, even though these may now be independent of the parent churches in Europe. There were those within the missionary bodies themselves who felt that insufficient care was being exercised with a view to enabling the mission-founded churches to organize their own life and hopefully come up with a more relevant form and content of Christian life and thought.

Perhaps the best-known expression of this hope for a more relevant missionary approach was Henry Venn's doctrine of the *"euthanasia* of a Mission" which visualized the church in Africa becoming a self-governing, self-supporting and self-extending church.[7] This doctrine does have the potential for bringing into being authentic structures to enable the mission-founded church to discover itself and to develop its true potential as a church set in a particular place. However, there is no *automatic* correlation between it and the creation of a truly local church. To "develop self-support and an ecclesiastical system suited to local circumstances in which African pastors were to carry increasing responsibility"[8] may not necessarily mean the development of relevant Christian thought. After all, the historic churches in many African countries are largely self-governing, self-support-ing (to varying degrees) and self-extending, yet they still tend to operate on the basis of Western theological ideas whose rele-vance to their local circumstances is questionable, to say the least.

By its life and thought the church in Africa, as in other third-world countries, has not sufficiently demonstrated its awareness of the advisability of ridding itself of the exclusivist tendencies which gave it birth. Of course, where a church is not aware of the exclusivist tendencies which brought it into being, it may itself practice exclusivist policies without being aware of their being such—practices, for example, such as prohibiting drum-ming at the wake-keeping for a member;[9] excluding those regarded as offenders, in particular polygamists, from the Lord's table, as many churches in Africa still do;[10] and being preoccu-pied with its rules and regulations rather than with matters of faith.[11] These practices illustrate the church's tendency to hedge itself off from "undesirable" people and ideas, the same attitude which characterized its formation in the days of Western mis-sions. In these and other ways the churches founded by the Western missionaries seem to be standing squarely in those the-ological traditions in which they were nurtured, even though by and large they are not directed from abroad.

It would be unfair, however, to give the impression that the inherited Westernism has gone unremarked and unchallenged within the church in Africa. This may be illustrated by reference, first, to the rise and growth of the independent churches.

THE INDEPENDENT CHURCHES

The motives underlying the establishment of the independent churches are varied indeed, ranging from petty jealousies within the leadership of an existing church at the one end of the scale, to issues of some theological significance at the other. As far as the latter is concerned it is acknowledged that many of these newer churches have come into being in reaction to the Westernism which the mission-founded churches so clearly display. Some leaders of these newer churches, as is well known, broke away from the historic churches because the leaders of the latter desired to maintain control, to the extent of insisting on the undesirability of accommodating traditional spirituality. It is an understatement to say that the independent churches have contributed immensely to the visibility of Christianity in Africa. Their mode of worship is often very different from that of the mission-founded churches, though not always in conscious reaction to them. Through their life and worship it has become clear to many Africans, in the rural as well as urban areas, that the Western lifestyle does not necessarily define what Christianity is all about. They are thus a challenge to the historic churches which, in some ways, seem more inclined now to adopt worship forms which would have been deeply frowned upon in the days of the early missionaries. Indeed, the worship life of these newer churches has not been without its effect on the historic churches. Music is one of the areas where the influence of these churches will be readily acknowledged.[12]

A second illustration of the desire to whittle down, if not totally eliminate, the Westernism which continues to exercise its effect upon the historic churches is in the moratorium call. In 1974 the All African Conference of Churches Assembly in Lusaka, Zambia, declared:

> To enable the African Church to achieve the power of becoming a true instrument of liberating and reconciling the African people, as well as finding solutions to economic and social dependence, one option as a matter of policy has to be a Moratorium on external assistance in money and personnel. We recommend this option as the only potent means of becoming truly and authentically ourselves while remaining a respected and responsible part of the Universal Church.[13]

Among the chief protagonists of the concept of a moratorium were John Gatu, then General Secretary of the Presbyterian

Church of East Africa, and Burgess Carr, then General Secretary of the All Africa Conference of Churches. The motive behind the call was a worthy one, to say the least: if the regular infusion of foreign personnel and money is making the African church less alive to its responsibilities, then this infusion must be stemmed. Of course, the situation with regard to missionaries and foreign financial aid differs from church to church. In some churches such aid, in personnel and cash, might be requested or offered for specific purposes; in others outside personnel have a significant presence, and through them comes a steady stream of money and equipment for the purpose of realizing the dreams of the foreign mission bodies for those African churches. Evidently a church which continues to be directed from outside is going to have an identity problem which, naturally, would not facilitate its theological maturing.

The moratorium call has not yielded any distinctive results, as far as one is able to judge. Apart from the fact that it "received an instinctive negative response from donors without a careful consideration of the issues involved,"[14] the churches in Africa themselves have not, by and large, determined to ensure that they are fully in control of their own movement towards maturity. That the All Africa Conference of Churches, having made this call, went on to appeal for money from outside Africa to enable it to construct its Nairobi headquarters is a measure of the lack of preparedness which made the call seem premature, even though it was well-intentioned.

Futhermore, though the influx of personnel and money from foreign donors can prevent a church from having a vision of the path which it could take given the cultural situation in which it finds itself, it must not be assumed that a church which raises personnel and funds locally for its own needs will necessarily and automatically develop a new understanding of itself. Empirical knowledge shows that is not a realistic equation. As observed earlier in connection with the *"euthanasia* of a Mission" doctrine, the historic churches in Africa are largely independent; they have African leadership, and in some of them more people offer themselves for leadership training than there are available resources. Many of them are flourishing in numbers, and the membership drive remains relentless. However, increasing numbers of personnel and members, and the availability of local funding notwithstanding, a church can still be prevented from having a true understanding of itself by the tenacity with which it clings to the past. There may yet be no urge to develop such Christian life and thought as would be distinctive in terms of a church's locus. To cite once again the story of the Methodist church, Ghana, which has been independent of the British Methodist church for almost three decades, this church's liturgy remains more or less as it was inherited; in many ways it breathes the spirit of British Methodism. The noises made in recent years regarding the possibility of stronger links being forged with other churches in the West may very well be a symptom of the church's tenuous control over its own life and thought, regarding the cultural reality in which it is situated.

Thus the moratorium call, vital as it is, serves, paradoxically, to underline the African church's failure to consider the *full* range of parameters of the development of a truly independent church, one which is truly alive to its responsibilities where it is found.

BIBLICAL INTERPRETATION

There is one area in the life of the African church, in particular, where the exclusivist tendencies which brought it into being have been given little or no attention, and that is biblical interpretation. The exclusivism which characterizes much of the biblical understanding of the relation between Israel's life and thought and that of other people has remained unevaluated as to its possible effect on mission as the African church endeavors to reach others in its own communities. Similarly biblical interpretation, having more or less remained as it was inherited from the missionary's home church, reinforces the exclusivist attitude in that it proceeds on the assumption that African life and thought have no part to play in the hermeneutical task. When Mbiti wrote in 1978 that "African Christianity has the Bible at its forefront, and the Bible is shaping much of its development both explicitly and implicitly"[15] he was perhaps giving African Christians more credit than they deserved. To be sure, the Bible is being read in the colonial languages, as well as in an increasing number of African languages, thanks to the efforts of a number of agencies funded from abroad; this is not to say, however, that such understanding of it prevails to enable it to play the right kind of role in theologizing. The truth of the matter is that the identification of the Bible as an important factor in theologizing has not kept pace with the exploration of its contents.

It is my considered opinion that ultimately it is in connection with the interpretation of the Bible that the African church will test its readiness to move away from the exclusivism in which it seems to be caught up. The Bible, as the primary source of the church's apprehension of God in Christ, must be so appropriated as for it to speak directly to the church. In the absence of such appropriation the Bible's true value will be seriously undercut, and the church's self-knowledge beclouded, to the point where its very existence is compromised.

As far as interpreting the Bible is concerned, a strongly literalist approach to it seems to have surfaced in Africa in recent decades, though it cannot be said to be peculiar to Africa. This mode of interpretation comes in two forms. According to one the Bible may be interpreted so as to give support to actions, policies, and institutions which are either contemplated or which have already been put into effect by a church. Sundkler provides us with evidence of this kind of interpretation as done by some of the independent churches in South Africa. As he put it, "Conformity with the Bantu heritage is really taken as the standard by which to judge Bible interpretation."[16] Thus to justify the practice of divination as a church ritual on the basis of Micah 4:13 (which really has nothing to do with divination) is merely to endeavor to find support for a practice which belongs to the traditional background of that church's members and thus cannot easily be abandoned.[17] Similarly, for a church to base its acceptance of polygamy on the fact that it was practiced by some of the giants of faith in Israel is to ignore the fact that polygamy was not the normal form of marriage in biblical times, even though it was considered acceptable.

This way of reading the Bible is unsatisfactory for two reasons. First, it is based on the failure to discern the meaning of the biblical text in its own ancient Near Eastern context. The two illustrations given above of this kind of interpretation show that in each case the cultural background of the Bible had been ignored. Secondly, this kind of biblical understanding makes no attempt to evaluate the traditional African religio-cultural world in order to make the interpretation reflect the essentials of African life and thought. To see Micah 4:13 as having to do with divination is to have established no real basis for interpreting the text meaningfully—any hermeneutical link with African life and thought would have been rendered non-existent. However one looks at it, this kind of biblical interpretation makes no pretense of throwing light on the biblical text, and it certainly does no justice to the basic African cultural presuppositions.

There is a related type of literalist interpretation which has found acceptance with increasing numbers of Christians in Africa; it must not be thought, though, that this is a peculiarly African development. As a matter of fact, its spread in Africa is not surprising considering the number of literalist preachers, both foreign and African (a significant number of the latter won their preaching spurs in America) who operate in Africa. Here, the interpreter does not use the Bible to justify institutions and ideas which are already favored, but instead starts with the desire to model Christian belief and practice strictly on practices, institutions, and ideas found or announced in the Scriptures, taking the plain sense of the text as automatically applicable in the interpreter's situation. With the increase in the charismatic ways of worship, especially but not exclusively in the new evangelical groups which have multiplied in African countries in the last decades, and which seem to beam their message at youth in particular, this way of reading the Bible has become widespread indeed. Of course, there is no doubting the fact that the plain sense of the text, by its very nature, can often have such an obviously overpowering force that it must be taken seriously. Thus Jesus' teaching on fasting which comes down hard on outward show will be considered to be of significance by many, if not all, Christians. It is God for whom worship is intended, not for one's self-glorification (Matt. 6:16-18). Similarly, hardly anyone would question Paul's wisdom when he recommends "whatever is true, whatever is honorable, whatever is just, whatever is pure, whatever is lovely, whatever is gracious" (Phil. 4:8).

It will be readily admitted, however, that life today has thrown up tensions that seem to call into question the value of the plain sense of a wide range of biblical passages. Most people would agree that loving the neighbor is an injunction which could enhance community feeling, peace, and development goals. However, there are Christians in parts of the world today whose loyalty to this exhortation is sorely tried daily in an atmosphere of downright hostility. It is hardly necessary to mention in this connection such countries as Ireland and South Africa. Yet even in these strife-torn areas there are many Christians who continue to show love for the neighbor, believing in its power to bring healing to the community. It can be imagined, however, that it will be difficult to adhere to Paul's injunction to slaves to "obey in everything those who are your earthly masters, not with eyeservice, as men-pleasers, but in singleness of heart, fearing the Lord" (Col. 3:22; cf. Eph. 6:5-8) in such a country as South Africa where the blacks who constitute the majority of the population have been confined by the white government to a comparatively small, and generally less hospitable, part of the country. It is true that Paul also exhorts masters to "treat your slaves justly and fairly, knowing that you also have a Master in heaven" (Col. 4:1; cf. Eph. 6:9), but what if the master does not behave as advised by Paul? And even if he does, is there any inherent justification anyway for the kind of master-servant relationship that lies at the back of Paul's injunction? There is yet another illustration of the problem, this time in connection with the Christian's relation to the secular authority; Paul devotes fully half of Romans 13 to this subject. Some of the instructions given there would be generally considered unexceptionable. When he exhorts his readers to "pay ... their dues, taxes to whom taxes are due, revenue to whom revenue is due" (Rom. 13:7) the wisdom of compliance will be readily admitted, for taxes give a government the means to provide such amenities as would enable the citizenry to live in some comfort. However, the literal sense of the rest of Romans 13:1-7 is going to strike readers as either palatable and supportive, or downright objectionable, depending on the reader's inclinations and circumstances. Paul's instructions were meant for those Christians in Rome who believed that Christians, *qua* Christians, did not have any need to obey any human authority since Christ was their king. Furthermore, it must be emphasized that Paul had in mind the kind of authority or state which was there to serve God's interests—not just any state.

This background to Paul's words has not prevented them from being misapplied. Thus it is possible for a secular authority to find in them justification for its rule. In this connection *The Kairos Document*, prepared by South African concerned Christians, has criticized the "blasphemous use of God's holy name" by the state.[18] However, even where a state does not make any claim to divine authority, the question will and does arise regarding whether or not Paul's words can have any relevance. Is anything owed to such a government other than civil disobedience? The history of Africa since the sixties witnesses to the repeated enactment of that tragic phenomenon—the military coup—often led by those whose only concern has been to safeguard their personal interests or those of the army. How seriously does a Christian take governments of this kind, considering that a military government is essentially illegitimate? Christians living under such a government are not likely to endeavor to look behind Paul's words to try to discover their background. And even if they did, they would still find these words justifying, even if indirectly, the questioning of an oppressive and incapable government, civilian or military, since such a government is the opposite of the kind which Paul had in mind. Would Paul have encouraged Christians to obey an iniquitous government?

In the light of the comments made so far about attitudes toward biblical interpretation certain questions arise which have a bearing upon our appropriation of the text of the Bible. These questions need to be given serious consideration in order to avoid a facile attitude toward the Scriptures. To begin with, if the plain sense of the text is not to be taken as necessarily applicable in a reader's situation, then the question arises as to the criteria by which one text would be adopted and another rejected. Many Christians in Africa are aware of the fact that until very recently women were prevented from entering the church to worship unless they had their heads covered (1 Cor. 11:5),[19] even though the church already accepted that there was nothing hindering women from praying and preaching. Thus the question arises of the grounds on which Paul's admonition "it is shameful for a woman to speak in church" (1 Cor. 14:35)[20] was set aside while churches continued to insist that a woman should cover her head in church. Parameters need to be established for the adoption or rejection of this or that biblical injunction or idea in order to avoid the charge of arbitrariness.

A second question, and one which is of fundamental importance, arises from the fact that a literalist interpretation often ignores the cultural reality in which the reader of the text is situated. This may be illustrated by reference to the so-called Jerusalem Council's decree (Acts 15:23-29)[21] which was issued to the Gentile Christians. On the basis of the literalist approach it may be argued that adherence to the injunction regarding the eating of blood (to mention just that) must be considered binding upon all those who become converts to Christianity. Now some African peoples do eat blood, not necessarily as part of ritual activity, but as sustenance; thus a specially prepared blood dish is regarded as a delicacy by some in Ghana. In my judgment, the question of whether or not Christians cease to be such on eating such a dish is easily answered. There can be no justification whatsoever for ignoring the cultural particularity of a convert by insisting on adherence to a regulation which has no identifiably Christian significance. As a matter of fact, this particular injunction arose from the church's Jewish religio-cultural background from which it sought, somewhat half-heartedly, to extricate itself. In this insistence, then, the cultural background of a convert would have been set aside for no valid reason.

What these comments indicate is that interpreting the Bible necessarily involves taking account of a person's or people's circumstances — cultural, socioeconomic, and political; without this dimension biblical interpretation becomes exclusivist.

Now in light of the possibility of the Bible's containing exhortations which may be considered inapplicable in particular circumstances, especially where the literalist type of interpretation is adopted, the question arises of whether or not this means that there is no *uniform* message in the Scriptures. It may be wondered whether it would not be more realistic to speak of messages, rather than the message of the Bible. To use fairly traditional terminology, is there a Word of God in the Scriptures to be acknowledged by all peoples and classes as being unquestionably valid? This is hardly the place to enter into the debate regarding whether or not there is such a Word, and how it might be characterized. The truth of the matter is that the Bible has given comfort to contending parties, comforting both the offender and the offended. The selling of one's fellow human beings into slavery; the terrible excesses committed by the Crusaders and the Spanish Inquisition enthusiasts; and in our time the policy of apartheid by which some are considered, for reasons of color, to be deserving of an inferior status in society— these and numerous other inequities have seemed right to their perpetrators on the basis of the Scriptures. Mosala has observed:

> The biblical truth that God sides with the oppressed is only one of the biblical truths. The other truth is that the struggle between Yahweh and Baal is not simply an ideological warfare taking place in the minds and hearts of believers, but a struggle between the God of the Israelite landless peasants and subdued slaves and the God of the Israelite royal, noble, landlord and priestly classes. The Bible is as rent apart by the antagonistic struggles of the warring classes of Israelite society as our life is torn asunder by the class divisions of our society.[22]

If the human experience is a necessary factor influencing Bible interpretation, then humanity's differing circumstances are going to result in different perceptions of what the Christian response to this or that situation is going to be.

From one point of view, then, it is possible to argue, as Mosala does, that it is unrealistic to insist on the concept of the Word of God if this is meant to be a denial of the conflicting strands of ideas in the Scriptures. From another point of view, however, it does not seem so unrealistic, and this is where one would take issue with Mosala. Ultimately, over the many and differing human circumstances, the warring attitudes and interests so clearly evidenced in the Bible, is written the message that an order could be realized which transcends the harsh and cruel vicissitudes of life. If there were no such possibility, then a passage such as Isaiah 58 which mirrors class struggles and differing attitudes to God and God's creation (the Scriptures insist that God created all peoples), and which teaches that each must care for the neighbor as God cares for all, would be nothing more than a gush of goodwill—and so would the death of Christ. From that point of view, then, I would argue that one should not hastily dismiss the concept of the Word of God as a Utopian universalization. This is not to deny, however, that Mosala is right in insisting on the need to recognize our distinctive human circumstances,[23] and their bearing upon Bible interpretation; interpretative realism requires this.

Two main conclusions may be drawn from the foregoing. First, interpreting the Bible calls for recognizing that it is a particular document—it arose out of the experiences of a particular people, the ancient Israelites. The writers of the books of the Bible did not have any people in mind but the people of Israel; even though the Bible gives us some information about some other peoples in the ancient world, it is Israel's story. This is the unavoidable starting point of biblical study and interpretation. The student of the Bible must first know the story of the Bible as it is, in its own religio-cultural context. This sounds deceptively simple, for in reality it is a difficult task, given the story of the evolution of the Bible. Great advances have been made, however; a number of techniques have been developed and brought to bear upon the explication of the text of the Bible, with the result that today there is a great deal more certainty about the text and more known about its meaning than was possible a generation ago. No exegete would get very far with the explication of the meaning of the Bible who did not first establish what the text was saying in its own historico-religious context.

There is a very important dimension of this which may not always have been taken into account. Only a small proportion of people in Africa can read the Bible in the colonial languages, and fewer still in the ancient languages, such as Hebrew and Greek. This underlines the importance of having the Bible in the local languages of Africa. A number of organizations working in Africa are translating the Bible and improving upon existing translations. A bad translation—and I know of such unhappy translations in African languages—is not going to enable one to appreciate what the biblical story actually is. That would deprive the reader of what is most basic to biblical interpretation — knowing what the text was saying to those readers for whom it was originally intended.

There should, however, be a clear awareness of the true purpose of knowing the text and what it is saying in its own historico-religious context. The purpose of this procedure is not simply to establish the antiquity of the text; it is not a question of putting the text into its ancient Near Eastern context and leaving it there, for that would in effect be labeling the Bible as an archaeological artifact, interesting but otherwise without life. That the Bible has sometimes been treated in this fashion is undoubtedly true. The determination of its particularity has been seen in some circles, consciously or unconsciously, as the ultimate goal of biblical exploration. This attitude has assumed a variety of shapes or forms in the history of Christianity, such as in that proclamation of the particularity of the text that ignores the unavoidable link that must be established between the text of the Bible and contemporary circumstances. Literalist interpretations belong to this category. When one has established the biblical story, the question then arises of its relevance for inquirers in light of their existential situation. If there were no possibility of establishing such a link between the then and the now, the Bible would be of much less value than one would think. As a matter of fact, the Bible itself invites its readers to find out for themselves the significance of faith, not only in the evidence it presents of the sometimes conflicting opinions of God's grace that arose when people sought to put into words their apprehension of the divine reality, but also in the *kerygma* with its invitation to respond to the divine offer. This response is made by living people, by flesh and blood.

The second conclusion to be drawn, therefore, is that the biblical exegete must come to the Bible armed with questions arising out of his or her own contemporary situation. In this connection it has been observed, "The exegetical work of every generation[24] reflects the current problems which have to be met in that particular period."[25] For the African the contemporary situation is a complex of religio-cultural ideas and customs, and socioeconomic and political uncertainties. I shall return to the explication of this.

For the moment it is to be noted that in expressing the need to bring existential questions to the Bible it is not being implied, as it might be thought, that the Bible has answers to all the questions being asked today in the contemporary African situation. Our world is much more complex than the world of the scriptural authors, and questions are being asked in Africa today which, given their particular setting, could hardly have been asked by the biblical writers in the same way. To be aware of this is to be saved from the error of reading more into the Bible text than is present in it. To be sure, some of the questions being asked today arise out of situations similar to those in ancient Israel, but it is a fact that we live in far more complex times.

In the African cultural situation this matter of approaching the Bible armed with existential questions assumes an added interest, though at the same time it becomes a potentially dangerous procedure. The African approach to the Bible cannot but take account of the fact which has been commented upon by a number of writers: there is much in common between the religio-cultural background of the Bible and African life and thought. In particular it has been demonstrated that there is much in the Old Testament which the African would find familiar.[26] Thus the various religious ideas and societal arrangements in the Bible enhance above all its human interest for the African who is enabled thereby to situate him- or herself in the complex of ideas and events which constitute the biblical story. The Western biblical scholar would almost certainly set little store by this "common" stock of ideas and customs, given the fact that Africa lies outside the cultural milieu of the ancient Near East. However, it has been shown that there are certain universal human reactions to situations and surroundings, and that being aware of these reactions can aid our understanding of their basic meaning and significance. Indeed, I believe that light could be thrown upon otherwise obscure biblical ideas and customs by reference to their "counterparts" in other traditions within and outside the ancient Near Eastern milieu.[27]

Paradoxically, a real danger—and one which some African Christians have been unable to avoid—lies in the very fact that the Bible does not present too much of a cultural barrier to the African. To accept uncritically the similarities between the Bible and African life and thought is to run the risk of misreading and therefore misinterpreting the Bible. When the *Ghanaian Weekly Spectator*[28] featured comments by a contributor to the effect that libation "is allowed in Christian circles," with the evidence given by the writer being references to libation in a number of Old Testament passages, the writer evidently failed to take account of the nature and significance of libation in the two differing contexts.

If, as argued above, African exegetes must come to the Bible armed with questions arising out of their existential situation, then two issues come up for consideration: in what does the African situation consist, and how is the relation between that and the explication of the Bible to be conceived if, as indicated already, it is not simply a matter of opening the pages of the Bible and finding neatly tailored answers?

AFRICAN LIFE, RELIGION, AND CULTURE

This is hardly the place for a detailed exposition of African life and thought. My purpose here is merely to highlight some of the main aspects of religion and life. No evaluation of African life would be meaningful without a realization of the fact that the African does not separate religion and life. Religion informs life in general insofar as there is no thought of a spiritual sphere which is unconnected with the physical; the two spheres are considered to overlap significantly. Hence, life is interpreted theologically with the people giving recognition to God and lesser divinities and spirits. Nothing occurs in the material world whose cause did not lie in the spiritual sphere. Not all the lesser divinities are approached as a means of reaching God; some being treated as ends in themselves. Nevertheless, a great deal of regard is given to God even though God may not be given regular worship, for God is seen as the creator who continues to control the world.

In many African societies the ancestors, who are held to belong to the spirit as well as the physical spheres, are paid a great deal of attention. They are believed to be custodians of morality as well as of the land, and they are approached not only in private rituals but also during community festivals when they are remembered and entreated on behalf of the living.

Festivals illustrate, perhaps above all societal institutions, the African reality of corporateness, for they bring together the living and the dead in the celebration of life. The concept of corporateness is one which has often been commented upon, though it is sometimes expressed so as to suggest, quite erroneously, that within this corporateness the individual has no room whatsoever to express individuality. Properly understood, the concept is an expression of the responsibility of the individual, both for oneself and for the community. Within this corporateness, then, patterns of interrelationships are recognized which ensure the community's equilibrium as well as the individual's integrity. Hence African societies have strict codes of behavior. The belief in God-given destiny notwithstanding, the principle of accountability is recognized at all levels of society. Just as the chief has a great deal of authority in the state, so the family head has considerable authority in the family, but these leaders would not be allowed to exercise authoritarian rule indefinitely. They are expected to remember that they bear responsibility for the individual in the family or state as well as for the group as a whole.

Much has happened in Africa over the last five decades or so to give rise to new questions, such as whether the issue of Christianity and African culture should be considered relevant at all, given the declared intention of African states to modernize. With African societies beginning to step boldly into modernity, should not the traditional ideas, customs, and institutions be outlawed on grounds of incompatibility with modernity? Or is coexistence possible? Questions of this kind have been asked, and they need to be seriously faced, for they have important implications for our inquiry. If it can be argued successfully that modernity — or whatever stage of it has been attained in Africa — is incompatible with African life and thought, then, of course, what has been said in this study about the desirability of Christianity seriously engaging African life and thought will seem fatuous. In reaction to this type of thinking I have suggested elsewhere that the ravages of the modern impinging forces notwithstanding, the traditional religio-cultural heritage has exhibited much resilience. Moreover, it is in the interests of Africans not to lose their identity, as they would surely do if they failed to take account of their religio-cultural heritage. Being who they are involves the realities of African languages, social customs, traditional religious presuppositions, societal interrelationships, and so forth, and it is imperative that the African's viewing of the wider world should be an endorsement of his or her integrity.

There is more to the African situation besides the religio-cultural facts. Thus the issue of church and state is increasingly exercising the minds of African Christians. The growing number of declarations, communiques, memoranda, and so forth, which have been issued in the post-colonial period by Christian councils of churches, Catholic bishops and other Christian bodies in many parts of Africa bears witness to this. In this connection the South African situation stands out, even though it must be acknowledged that the oppressive measures carried out by the white South African government are often matched by the brutality perpetrated by black African governments against their own citizens. And with the increasing resort by rulers to violent methods arises the issue of the Christian and violence: does the Christian adopt or encourage the adoption of violent means against wicked regimes? Is violence unavoidable in certain circumstances?

Some of the pressing issues today concern military coups which have become a scourge in our time; they have caused a great deal of concern, for invariably they have brought oppression, brutality, and disillusionment in their train. In some countries under military rule security consciousness and militarization are important factors causing disaffection among the general populace, because the security goals sought by the rulers involve considerable expenditures that hinder the government in developing programs to alleviate social stress. It may be argued that this is not a peculiarly African problem, for military build-ups by the more affluent countries often siphon off funds from other programs of immediate material benefit to the people. All the same, the African situation, compounded as it is by many other deleterious factors (such as scarcity of foreign exchange, and populations which are growing faster than those of other continents), involves deprivation and suffering which in fact works against the momentum of development.

Lastly, mention should be made of the ease with which some African governments adopt political ideologies from non-African countries. The questions raised by this are not very different from those being raised in relation to the adoption of a Western-oriented form of Christianity. An ideology developed in a specific cultural situation can hardly be expected to fit meaningfully into another cultural context; on the contrary, it can become a source of much confusion and short-sightedness relative to the real needs and problems of a people.

AN AFRICAN APPROACH TO THE SCRIPTURES

It is evident from this brief exposition of the African situation that African exegetes could be overwhelmed by the variety of questions with which they might arm themselves as they approach the Scriptures. The issue that now arises is how the prevailing situation and the Scriptures could be related with a view to interpreting the Scriptures for one's own circumstances: how may one discern possible answers to questions which arise out of the human situation?

The question just posed sounds simple enough: exegetes seek answers to questions and they confront the Scriptures in which they discover apparently the same or similar themes in this or that verse, and conclude that this must provide unerring guidance. The point has already been made that it would be wrong to suppose that the Bible has answers to all the questions being asked today. Moreover, to adopt this interpretative procedure is invariably to read more into the biblical text than there actually is, thus making the Scriptures endorse human desires willy-nilly. In this regard, then, the misinterpretation of Scripture becomes a distinct possibility, and a standard of relationships, actions, and reactions could be endorsed which has nothing to do with the scriptural material. Moreover, every culture has its own answers to situations that arise within it or in relation to it. Thus the adoption of the method of interpretation whereby the biblical verse or passage is uncritically matched with a contemporary life situation implies an uncritical acceptance of the answers which a culture itself provides to the questions being asked. It is important not only to discover the cultural answers to questions arising from the prevailing circumstances, but also to question those answers. Without this questioning the temptation to make the Bible endorse those answers could be overwhelming. Where the Bible has been made to play this role, it has not really been a constitutive factor in the interpretative process. No cultural given can be exempted from such critical appraisal.

Similarly, just as a critical attitude toward the answers provided within the cultural situation must of necessity be adopted, so the scriptural answers, or what would appear to be such, must be critically viewed. It has already been shown that there are certain ideas in the Scriptures which, viewed in relation to certain specific human circumstances, cannot but be considered unworkable. Of course, the thought of the Scriptures being critiqued is bound to strike some as unacceptable, especially when it is denied that the authors of the biblical books, men (and women?) who were compelled by their faith in God to write, were nevertheless people of their times, whose understanding of God and God's ways was also shaped by the cultural, socioeconomic, and political circumstances of their societies. The differing attitudes to non-Israelites surveyed in the first chapter makes this clear. Moreover, the point cannot be made more strongly that the questions being asked today have their own particularity—they did not concern the writers of the biblical books as such.

In the light of these comments one might reiterate the question posed above, and ask on what basis interpretative insights relative to a particular society's questions should be considered acceptable. My intention here, I must hasten to explain, is not to provide detailed pointers—if indeed it were possible to do so—for that would require a study by itself. All I am attempting here is to make two statements which are broad enough to encompass a variety of ideas and hopefully encourage a closer investigation of the issues involved.

The first statement is one which has received much attention from the exponents of liberation theology, and which will continue to have to be heard because of its tendency to be suppressed, for a variety of reasons, in many parts of the world. Any biblical interpretation which fails to endorse a person's or a people's inherent dignity hardly deserves to be taken seriously. In this regard one might mention discrimination (racial, on grounds of religion, color, and so forth), the denial of one's cultural identity and worth, educational and other policies which cause alienation, all forms of exploitation, and starvation. A Christian could hardly be satisfied with any interpretative insight which implied unquestioning acceptance of evil situations of this kind, or worse still, which encouraged them. Such an insight would surely contradict biblical teaching on creation which, among other things, shows that our differing cultural particularities are in accordance with God's will.[29] What is being suggested here is not, on the one hand, simply an automatic endorsement of all the humanity of a particular people, for that would mean a blind acceptance of the answers offered by that people's culture. On the other hand, I do not mean to gloss over the fact that Scripture, at another level, does not always endorse the principle of a people's humanity and dignity as being non-negotiable. Thus not only do we have such an episode as the treacherous elimination of Naboth (1 Kings 21:1ff.), but also we have the fact of ritual discrimination, which Jesus subverted when he touched the leper (Mark 1:40-41). If I have expressed here a preference for accepting the humanity and dignity of all persons and peoples, it is because the fundamental nature of God's creatorship makes human beings, wherever they are found, God's.

There is good reason for first bringing up this matter of human dignity, for this is precisely the area in which exclusivist attitudes showed most clearly in the early days of missions, both in the early church and in Africa in modern times where the culture of the people was largely ignored at best, or suppressed at worst. Similarly, the excesses of our modern times associated with discrimination in a wide range of areas of life have often sorely tested Christian obedience in many parts of the world. The Bible has been used to oppress and disadvantage people. Any talk of Christianity, therefore, must take account of the flesh and blood for whose sake Christ died.

The second statement concerns the death of Christ. The

Scriptures make it clear that Christ died that we might be made anew, his death freeing us from all that puts a distance between us and God. Different parties would have viewed his death differently—as that of a criminal who had been overtaken by justice, or as that of an innocent person against whom trumped-up charges had been brought, and so forth. Whatever one might say about it, it is made clear in the Scriptures that Christ's death was to bring about healing—to repair the broken relationship between God and us, and thereby engender a new level of interrelationships in society. After all, in the events surrounding that death we see several qualities which the world seldom displays: fortitude (Mark 15:23), forbearance (Luke 23:34), care for others (John 19:26), and many more. At the same time, the death of Christ represents God's implacable hostility to sin—God in Christ would not compromise with evil. Thus Christ's death becomes a mirror in which we might see God's determination to reach us in order to restore our true nature, not only as individuals, but also as one people.

An interpretation which fails to take account of these two statements and their implications is likely to founder in the sea of needless speculation and inveigling personal desires and wishes.

Much of what follows now will illustrate the kind of interpretative exercises that could be done having in mind the African existential reality. The comments made here on these three passages are not meant to exhaust their possibilities; they are simply aimed at highlighting that dimension which encourages their particularization.

Hebrews 1:1-2

> In many and various ways God spoke of old to our fathers by the prophets; but in these last days God has spoken to us by a Son, whom God appointed heir of all things, through whom also God created the world.

This is perhaps one of the best known New Testament passages. Its significance becomes apparent when one considers the three time-references contained in it; in commenting on this passage the tendency has been to concentrate on the first two of these references, to the virtual exclusion of the third, without which consideration the passage is robbed of a vital aspect of its relevance.

In the first time-reference the writer draws attention to the days *of old* when God spoke by the prophets. This prophetic work was a preparation for the time to come when God would speak more "authentically"; thus not only was the prophetic activity a preparation but also it was inadequate as far as the disclosure of God's will is concerned.

The second time-reference is in the phrase *in these last days*: God has now spoken through God's son Jesus. This *now* is of crucial importance, for the Christian faith hinges on the fact of the Messiah who comes from God to save humanity.

The third time-reference is, in my judgment, seldom appreciated as to its true possibilities. This is expressed in two phrases, *the heir of all things*, and *through whom also God created the world*. This time-reference takes us up to the creation; not only is Christ the agent of creation, but also in him *all things* cohere. This reference becomes the means of sharpening the first time-reference, for it enables the reader to set the reference to *our fathers* and *the prophets* of Israel against the background of a time-depth which diminishes its particularity. In other words, on the basis of the third time-reference it becomes possible for the African exegete to see in this passage an invitation to fit into it the story of the African striving after spiritual reality, so that *our fathers* becomes for the African *his* or *her* fathers as well. The reference to creation which, as already indicated, is the ground of our oneness in God, invites the exegete to particularize the text in the way suggested here. In so proceeding the exegete would not have tampered with the story in its own historico-religious context; however, the story would have been made the basis, quite legitimately, for reflecting upon the reality of all peoples having been created by God who must be presumed to be involved in their life and thought.

It is a fact that in our time many more Christians than ever before seem inclined toward the conviction that there is only one God of the whole earth whom the different peoples of the world are seeking to approach in the particularities of their dif-

fering life circumstances. This conviction, I would suggest, is
nothing but an explication of the Hebrews passage. Thus in 1967
a consultation of African theologians drew up a statement which
read in part:

> We recognise the radical quality of God's self-revelation
> in Jesus Christ; and yet it is because of this revelation that
> we can discern what is truly of God in our pre-Christian
> heritage: this knowledge of God is not totally discontinu-
> ous with our people's traditional knowledge of Him.[30]

This statement contains the important implication that biblical
exposition begins with the recognition of a theological continuity
between the Bible and the African religio-cultural heritage, an
implication which calls for giving this religio-cultural heritage its
rightful place in the African Christian's appropriation of the
Christian faith.

Exodus 28:2-3

> And you shall make holy garments for Aaron your brother,
> for glory and for beauty. And you shall speak to all who
> have ability, whom I have endowed with an able mind, that
> they make Aaron's garments to consecrate him for my
> priesthood.

From the African point of view this passage is not without
interest, for it links up with the point made in my brief exposition
of the African situation that in the African understanding religion operates in all spheres of life; to distinguish between the
sacred and the secular is to do harm to the full dimensions of
either of them. The Exodus passage quoted above implies the
same kind of understanding. It is only the occasional commentary that draws out the significance of the passage on the basis
of the ancient Near Eastern concept of a nexus binding religion
and life.

Two phrases in the passage are crucial for understanding its
meaning. The phrase *all who have ability* is a translation of the
Hebrew which literally reads *all who are wise of heart*, and *able*

mind in the Hebrew original is *a spirit of wisdom*. Thus the passage speaks of the tailor's skill as a demonstration of wisdom which is seen as coming from God—God is the one who has endowed the craftsmen with this wisdom.

Now in the ancient world crafts and trades of various kinds were learned through family and guild traditions, with the prospective artisans serving a period of apprenticeship. In view of this it may be considered odd that the passage under discussion should speak of the tailor's art as being God-inspired; in reality, however, this is an expression of the sovereignty of God. The Old Testament in particular contains various statements of God's involvement in the life and pursuits of people. It is for this reason that the practice of tampering with other people's plots of land is decried; not only is it anti-social, but it is also taking on God, the "redeemer" of the disadvantaged (see Prov. 23:10-11; cf. Deut. 19:14 and 27:17). Similarly, the belief is expressed that the farmer carries out agricultural functions in accordance with God's instructions (Isa. 28:24f.). This last reference is of more than passing interest for it links up with African ideas quite neatly. Thus even though the African belief in the Earth goddess brings African ideas closer to the Canaanite belief in the land as infused with divinity, yet the African belief exists that it is God who makes the land fruitful through life-giving rain.[31]

That Western exegetes seldom look at these and similar passages in this way (thus missing the opportunity to bring out their importance for understanding the role of religion in life) is largely a reflection of the Western lifestyle. Further, the African church's adoption of Western theological patterns and content in training full-time workers has prevented African students of the Bible from appreciating a characteristic of biblical life and thought. This process not only underlines the human interest in the Bible, but also serves as a corrective to the Western expression of Christianity which ignores the biblical idea that the faith-conviction must inform a person's total life.

Luke 8:22-24

> One day he got into a boat with his disciples, and he said to them, "Let us go across to the other side of the lake."

So they set out, and as they sailed he fell asleep. And a
storm of wind came down on the lake, and they were filling
with water, and were in danger. And they went and woke
him, saying, "Master, Master, we are perishing!" And he
woke and rebuked the wind and the raging waves; and they
ceased, and there was a calm.

The gospels contain a number of accounts of Jesus' power
over demons. These accounts associate demons with desert
areas and cemeteries, and may note the change wrought in a
person who was possessed (calm instead of being wild in appear-
ance and behavior). But it is not only human beings who may
be possessed; the sea or lake, for example, may be thought of
as a distinct personality, though, as in our passage, one full of
evil and destructive forces. Indeed, people in both Old and New
Testament times believed that the whole of nature was full of
evil, so that Deborah and Barak could sing of the storm which
incapacitated the chariots of the hostile Canaanite forces, thus
demonstrating the power of God (Judg. 5:1ff.). Similarly, Jesus
"rebuked the wind and the raging waves; and they ceased, and
there was a calm." Ideas of this kind will be found familiar in
Africa, and yet they are rarely, if ever, made to inform the thinking of African Christians relative to questions of healing.

Until recently, hardly any of the historic churches openly
expressed an interest in the ministry of healing, a hangover from
these churches' missionary past when the emphasis was on Western medicine. Healing services are known to have been held in
some historic churches, not, however, in obedience to any official
church injunction, but on the basis of particular ministers' inclinations. Beetham is right in questioning the historic churches'
failure to exercise such a ministry.[32] The independent churches
in Africa, in contrast, seem fully committed to this ministry, a
fact which, at least partly, explains their popularity.

It is clear that healing accounts, such as the one quoted
above, enshrine an understanding of causation and dynamism
which should excite the African exegete, for they evidently
encourage their particularization by reference to the African
situation.

Many more passages could be cited and explored to illustrate the variety of questions with which the exegete could confront the Bible, and the kinds of answers which might be elicited. This, however, should not be necessary, partly because a considerable number of passages would need to be cited in order to illustrate adequately the variety of questions and answers which arise, and partly because my intention here is a limited one: to underline the fundamental fact of the need to particularize the biblical text in relation to current existential circumstances. In any case, from comments already made it will have become clear, for example, that the words of Paul could be a veritable treasure trove — as well as a minefield — of interpretative possibilities in the African context.

In making these comments I do not intend to suggest that the theological explorations being done in Africa and elsewhere in the Third World have shown no interest in the Bible as a document which reveals something of the mind of God for people at particular times and in particular places. It hardly needs to be pointed out that theologies of liberation have drawn heavily upon the exodus motif in the Scriptures, and so have independent churches in South Africa. This is understandable, for the exodus does exemplify God's desire to free the disadvantaged from oppression and to restore their humanity. However, important as the exodus motif is, it is of greater importance that one's understanding of the Bible, in all its parts, should be influenced by one's societal circumstances.

In this connection one might draw a distinction between two levels of biblical understanding — the macro and the micro levels. By the macro level is meant seeing the Bible from the point of view of a message whose distinctiveness is glaring and indisputable. The exodus is such a message, for it is exemplified not only in a particular event, but also in the various vicissitudes of Israel's history — in their defeats and their refusal, under God, to succumb to forces of oppression; hence the reference to the message of the exodus that runs through the Old Testament, from the exodus event to the resumption of life in Palestine following the return from the Babylonian exile, and through the New Testament, from the futile attempt to eliminate the baby Jesus to his victory over death. It is well known that there have been a variety of formulations of what is considered at the macro level to be the message of the Scriptures; different writers have espoused different formulations in accordance with their reading of the Scriptures. The exodus motif has struck the downtrodden as being most meaningful for the obvious reason that it speaks to their situation. Thus at the macro level, the possibility of a "global" assessment of the Scriptures arising from the nature of one's circumstances is clearly indicated.

However, the possibility of one's circumstances shaping one's appropriation of the Scriptures becomes even more compelling when the Scriptures are considered at the micro level, by which is meant the level of the different books and, more especially, the differing ideas making up the books. It is a fact that sometimes conflicting ideas may be presented in the same books, as we discovered in connection with Micah 4:1-5. Considered at this level, then, the Scriptures are found to be overflowing with a profusion of ideas some of which, as already shown, might not find acceptability in particular cultural, socioeconomic, and political circumstances.[33] Ideally, one would have wished for things to be such that the macro and micro levels of biblical exploration would at all times and in all places yield the same kind of understanding. However, the realities of humanity's diverse circumstances, coupled with the variety of biblical ideas, cannot always ensure this. Almost certainly, this is bound to be interpreted by some to mean a dismembering of Christian solidarity; to me, however, it would be bringing realism into that solidarity, for Christ died for all.

I am deeply convinced that, when all is said and done, biblical interpretation of the kind being advocated here is most essential for ridding Christianity of the exclusivist attitude which has been such a regular companion of mission. This attitude was fostered initially by the sending churches in the West, and now fostered, often more unconsciously than consciously, by the receiving churches, with their readiness to see the Bible through the eyes of the Western Christians who, quite naturally, interpret the Bible in the light of their own circumstances. To interpret the Bible in the African church's own existential circumstances would be for the church to uproot that element which is at the core of the inherited exclusivist character of Christianity. It would be underscoring the church's true character, for as the

Bible speaks of the vicissitudes of life before God the creator, so is the church to bear witness to God before men and women whom God has created. Thus one of the true marks of a church should be that under the guidance of the Spirit it will have learned to relate the Bible to its own circumstances as a community of believers set amid wider communities with which it must necessarily interact. It is most decidedly not the mark of a church that it should be a ghetto of believers.

6

Conclusion

This investigation of Christianity in the former mission areas, with special reference to Africa, reinforces certain aspects of the theological quest going on in Africa, the significance of which may not have been sufficiently recognized. While this has not been an exhaustive investigation, the various leads followed in the preceding chapters suggest the views expressed in recent decades by advocates of innovative theological thinking. The present stage of the discussion, which is beginning to be marked by some theological formulations,[1] comes in the wake of certain developments which will be stated briefly here as a preliminary to highlighting some of the views which have been aired regarding the factors which should influence the rethinking of the Church's heritage.

It is possible to delineate certain broad stages in the wrestling with Christian life and thought which has gone on in Africa, especially in the last four decades or so. In the late forties and early fifties, discussions on the subject were fairly general; they hardly ever went beyond the articulation of the bare and broad issues regarding the ostensibly un-African face of Christianity. Similarly—and not surprisingly—recommendations regarding how to remedy the situation tended to be limited to external ritual and related adjustments which, though it was not stated as such, would give some authentic color to Christianity. It was not realized, apparently, that this remedial procedure would leave the central issue unaffected – the inability of Christian theology to address the African situation in its entirety. As a matter of fact, at this stage the church's attitude toward colonialism and all that it implied was hardly questioned. Thus, not surprisingly, for those who gave the matter of Christianity's apparent inappropriateness any thought, the way forward seemed to lie in what was evidently a limited engagement, as it were, between Christianity and African religion and culture. In practical terms, the solutions recommended were largely of the adaptionist variety. Then, in the wake of the increasing number of university departments of theology/religious studies which teach and seriously investigate African traditional religion, more weighty questions began to be asked. Can it be said that God has revealed himself in this religion too? If God has, then there is a compelling reason to make much more of traditional spirituality than simply to isolate aspects of it for purposes of adaptation. It was this more radical questioning which gave birth to the expression of "African" theology. This term was meant to represent the new outlook on the matter at issue, as well as the eventual theological formulation which would do justice to African circumstances as a whole.

As yet, however, the question of what factors should influence the new theologizing remained unclear, beyond the identification of Christianity and African life and thought. It had simply been assumed that theologizing would be done on the basis of inherited Christianity and the African religio-cultural tradition. It was another decade or so before other factors were identified, notably the Scriptures. Regrettably, the exploration of the Bible, beyond the literalist kinds of interpretation, has yet to become a significant fact in the African church. As I have shown, there is a variety of possibilities with regard to the investigation of the Scriptures, considering their interpretation for one's times and circumstances. The ideas explored in the preceding chapter pose a challenge to the theological investigator which has yet to be taken up with sufficient seriousness.

The first two chapters of this study underline, among other things, the fact that the Bible is the story of a people on a journey into the knowledge of God. The people of Israel were seekers after God, and different glimpses of God's ways were obtained in accordance with the enquirers' varying existential circumstances; hence the variety of views and attitudes found in the Old Testament. To be sure, whatever religious attitude was adopted in any particular situation would have been firmly defended, but on the basis of one's own understanding of God's demands. Thus to look upon the Old Testament as giving a *finished* understanding of God—whatever that might mean—is to claim more for the Old Testament than the documents comprising it would lead us to do. This is not to say that the Old Testament does not contain insights of eternal value, such as its repeated warning against treating others as if they did not matter before God. After all, the Old Testament as a whole sees the world as God's—God has made it and all that is in it, and this fact calls for obedience to God's providential will. Likewise, the New Testament is a collection of documents which illustrate a journey into faith. The differing attitudes surveyed, like those of the Old Testament, show that the human circumstances of the various actors played a part in defining what was seen as God's guidance for them. The incarnation, of course, becomes the permanent context in which to view the various understandings of God's ways found in the documents, for indeed there is no uniformity in this regard. In one sense, then, the incarnation both validates and unifies the various views of God; in another sense, however, it judges them, especially when they do injustice to the conviction of God's loving concern for humanity.

Given the nature of the contents of the Bible, a careful study of its contents is called for. If the Bible does not constitute a finished quest for God, with the Holy Spirit as the ever-present guide as Christ assured his disciples he was, then students of the Bible, of every country and in every generation, join a band of seekers, and the Bible becomes for them not only the story of how others understood something of God in the realities of their life circumstances, but also a staging ground for the exploration of what acknowledging God in Christ means. Thus it is not a matter of choosing between discerning a message, on the one hand, and on the other following leads provided by insights revealed in and through specific concrete human situations and experiences. That would be hiding away from the full range of ideas which would encourage the raising of those theological questions that could in turn enrich theological formulations. A genuine theological understanding of the Bible calls for the appreciation and investigation of its captivating dialectic.

If in approaching the Bible the reader is joining a search for meaning, then it is to be expected that he or she would not only investigate its variety of voices, but also progress beyond those voices, under the guidance of the Spirit. Human situations are seldom constant, which largely explains the un-uniform nature of the biblical picture itself. Thus the Bible itself points to a pilgrimage in which it joins hands with one's spatial and temporal circumstances to constitute a guiding partner, and whose ultimate goal is not a static but an ever renewable sense of security of Christ.

The investigation of the Bible should of necessity issue from biblical commentaries, since these are an important aid to theologizing, especially where they take account of what has been described here as the biblical dialectic, linking it up with the existential human situation. The availability of such commentaries would broaden the discussion's base, saving our theologizing from being "specialist" in the sense that the majority of the theologian's fellow church members, especially those who are simply involved in periodic worship and accept this as the acid test of their Christian affiliation, may not be willing or able to raise questions or contribute toward the concerns of the "specialist." In particular, it is surprising that the decades of discussions on theologizing in the African context have not affected the great majority of the ordained functionaries of the church. Generally speaking, the seminaries and bible colleges where they would have been trained operate curricula that do not allow for these concerns. Even where such concerns are articulated and discussed, the biblical commentaries with which the students investigate the biblical material may not offer truly relevant help. Many of the available Western commentaries are excellent studies, but the fact remains that no matter how searching these might be, their insights are not always sufficiently earthed in the kind of circumstances with which the student might identify. Thus theological speculation and formulation in Africa stand a fair chance of becoming totally elitist, the preserve of a few, among whom may be numbered not more than a handful of the church's ordained ministers.

It is of the nature of a quest of this kind that the human particularity should be respected. To ignore the actualities of the human experience is to reduce the eternalness of the Scriptures, for one would have tied them solely to an age gone for ever. It would be burying the Scriptures with the past.

There is another aspect of the theological task which arises from this study, and which needs to be given more attention than it has received hitherto, especially by a church which is at the initial stages of assuming responsibility for its own life and thought; and that is the genesis and development of the doctrinal teaching of the church, the importance of which can be easily overlooked. In recent years a number of African theologians have acknowledged that the life and thought of the church, from its beginnings in Palestine till the present, are relevant to theologizing, but little has otherwise been said in explication.

Mission churches and African theological institutions are inheritors of a great variety of doctrinal developments which have come about through the ages and are read in works on the history of doctrine: they are also inheritors of specific denominational theological insights associated with the sending churches in Europe and America. Hence theological thought in Africa has come under the influence of a weighty store of theological reflections. The university department of religious studies/theology and the seminary/bible college become the setting where the inherited theological formulations are presented, usually as "gospel." Seminary students are taught to consider the denominational "emphases" as an unavoidable means of looking at God and the meaning of our human existence. The references made in this study to some Western theological scholars make no pretense of being extensive, but they do suggest the need to thoroughly reexamine theological ideas which have been handed down, particularly the denominational "emphases" which define denominational purity. My own experience is that an unimaginative attachment to these so-called emphases can have a paralyzing effect, shutting out other more realistic theological possibilities. Thus in my *Theology in Africa*[2] I suggest that inherent in John Wesley's understanding of holiness is the possibility of a sharp distinction being drawn between God and the world. The new theological emphasis emanating from the Third World is based, quite rightly, on the rejection of such a separation.

Thus there are both positive and negative reasons for paying close attention to the universal church's theological developments. The positive aspect is, as already implied, that these reflections are part of the worldwide church's heritage, representing attempts by men and women to understand the wisdom of God in Christ in the light of who they were — men and women of their own times and circumstances. Some of these theological insights can undoubtedly be relevant, given the fact that our human situations and reactions may not always be so very different. However, inasmuch as the human circumstances *can* differ, and often differ drastically, the inherited theological formulations must sometimes be viewed with caution. Their worth must be tested in the light of one's own circumstances. The former mission areas are especially in mind here, for it is in these areas, in particular, that the adoption of theological ideas developed elsewhere tends to be total. The necessary evaluation is seldom done, mainly because those to whom these reflections are presented lack the tools for such evaluation. More often than not — that is, if the matter is given any thought at all — the received theological ideas become the basis of adaptionist procedures, which assume the inviolability of those ideas.

While it must be admitted that adaptionism is capable of enriching certain areas of church life, such as worship, the call for its rejection as the means of achieving the goal of a radical rethinking of what God in Christ means in the African existential situation has much to recommend it. It cannot constitute the sole, or even the main, theological procedure. It is not of the nature of this theological method that it should result in such reshaping as is being actively advocated.

Any theological procedure which makes the theological quest nothing more than a regurgitation of inherited thinking, thus in effect leaving the latter intact, is entrenching exclusivism, and the church's mission remains uncompleted.

Exclusivism is a challenge to be met with imagination, for the sake of Christ's mission.

Notes

INTRODUCTION

1. Austin Flannery, O.P. (ed.), *Vatican II, The Conciliar and Post Conciliar Documents* (Leominster: Fowler Wright Books, 1981; Collegeville, Minn.: Liturgical Press, 1983), 824.

1. JEWISH ATTITUDES TOWARD OTHER PEOPLES UP TILL THE TIME OF CHRIST

1. R. E. Clements, "Covenant and Canon in the Old Testament" in Richard W.A. McKinney (ed.), *Creation, Christ and Culture* (Edinburgh: T. & T. Clark, 1976), 7.

2. Among the shorter references to Amenophis (or Akhenaton) are L. H. Gröllenberg's *Shorter Atlas of the Bible* (Nashville: Thomas Nelson, 1961 [reprinted]), 44, and Cyril Eastwood, *Life and Thought in the Ancient World* (London: University of London, 1964), 105.

3. H. Ringgren, *Israelite Religion* (Philadelphia: Fortress Press, 1966), 39.

4. The reference here is not to the worship of Aton, the Sun Disc; Egyptian myths are replete with divine beings, Reh the Sun being one of these mythological gods.

5. Martin Noth, *Exodus* (Philadelphia: Westminster Press, 1962), 163.

6. G. R. Driver, "Birds in the Old Testament" in *Palestine Exploration Fund Quarterly* 87 (1955): 5-20.

7. Werner Forster, *Palestinian Judaism in New Testament Times* (Edinburgh: Oliver and Boyd, 1964), 145.

8. Luther was certainly right when he rendered the Hebrew *adham* as *Menschen* (mankind) in German.

9. See my "Continuity and Discontinuity Between the Old Testa-

ment and African Life and Thought" in K. Appiah-Kubi and S. Torres (eds.), *African Theology en Route* (Maryknoll: Orbis Books, 1979), 95ff.

10. J. Gray, *The Legacy of Canaan* (Leiden: E.J. Brill, 1957), 140ff., and H. Ringgren, *Israelite Religion*, 175-77.

11. I.e., discounting the Abimelech episode (Judg. 9:1ff.).

12. S.W. Baron, *A Social and Religious History of the Jews* (New York: Columbia University Press, 1962), 127.

13. A. Lods, *The Prophets and the Rise of Judaism* (London: Routledge and Kegan Paul, 4th printing 1961), 275.

14. The Ammonites (Jer. 49:1-6); the Moabites (Zeph. 2:8 and Ezek. 25:8-11); and Edom, the bitterest enemy (Ezek. 25:12-14).

15. See especially Deutero-Isaiah and Jonah.

16. See p. 20-21 above.

17. The Kenites were a Midianite clan.

18. Yehezkel Kaufmann, *The Religion of Israel* (London: George Allen & Unwin, 1961), 301; see 2 Kings 5:1ff.

19. Quoted by Emil Schürer, *The History of the Jewish People in the Age of Jesus Christ*, a new English edition (Edinburgh: T. & T. Clark Ltd., 1986), vol. III, 161.

20. Schürer, *History of the Jewish People*, 176.

21. Ibid., 174.

2. THE EARLY CHURCH: QUESTIONS AND ATTITUDES

1. See Samuel Sandmell, *A Jewish Understanding of the New Testament* (Hoboken, NJ: Ktav, 1974; London: SPCK, 1977), 179-80.

2. L. T. Johnson, *The Writings of the New Testament* (Minneapolis, MN: Augsburg Fortress; London: SCM Press, 1986), 203.

3. See E.P. Sanders, *Jesus and Judaism* (Philadelphia: Fortress Press, 1985), Part Two.

4. K. Lake and H. Cadbury, *The Beginnings of Christianity, Part 1: The Acts of the Apostles* (London: Macmillan, 1933).

5. C. W. Carters and R. Earle, *The Acts of the Apostles* (Grand Rapids: Zondervan, 1973).

6. Lake and Cadbury, *The Beginnings of Christianity*.

7. *Haereses* 1, 26:3.

8. G. B. Caird, *A Commentary on the Revelation of St. John the Divine* (London: A. and C. Black, 1966).

9. Lake and Cadbury, *The Beginnings of Christianity*.

10. It is generally recognized that the speeches in The Acts were composed by Luke himself, though on the foundation of such information and material as to make them fair representations of the view

and ideas of those to whom the speeches are attributed.

11. Luke could have found strong Old Testament support for this attitude to tradition in Jeremiah's teaching of the future of religion; see John Skinner, *Prophecy and Religion* (Cambridge: Cambridge University Press, 1951), 165ff.

12. See the summary of this in Acts 7:51-53.

13. Probably from the Greek form of the Hebrew word which translates as Messiah.

14. Stephen Neil, *Through Many Eyes* (Guildford: Lutterworth, 1976), 122.

15. The Acts refers to the town in question as "Antioch in Pisidia." Actually this Antioch was not in Pisidia; it was a Roman colony, the most important town in southern Galatia, near the Pisidian border.

16. Cf. Rom. 1:20.

17. F.F. Bruce, *The Acts of the Apostles* (Wheaton, IL: Tyndale Press, 1951).

18. *The Interpreter's Bible*, vol. IX (Nashville, TN: Abingdon, 1954).

19. *deisidaimonesteros*.

20. See King James Version.

21. The argument that this would not be characteristic of Paul can hardly be sustained, for Paul does not view pagan religious attitudes in as positive a light as one might think, beyond the affirmation that there is one God, the evidence of whose existence is there for all to see. We shall return to this in connection with Galatians, p. 44 below.

22. Compare the worship of the Anlo of Ghana who in prayer would make a reference to spirit powers in general for the same reason, even though they might have particular spirits in mind. See C. R. Gaba, "Prayer in Anlo Religion" in *Orita* 11, 2 (December 1968).

23. N. B. Stonehouse, *Paul before the Areopagus and Other New Testament Studies* (Wheaton, IL: Tyndale Press, 1957), 18f.

24. Not in a pantheistic sense; contrast *The Interpreter's Bible*, vol. IX, 236.

25. Cf. Rom. 1:18ff.

26. J. L. Martyn, in *Michigan Quarterly Review* XXII, 3 (Summer 1983): 221ff.

27. Ibid., 221.

28. Ibid., 223.

29. Ibid., 227.

30. Cf. Gal. 1:7.

31. Ibid., 228.

32. Ibid., 235.

33. The accuracy of this incident has been doubted. It has been

argued that in Galatians 5:11 Paul protests against the rumor that he preaches circumcision; see G. Bornkamm, "The missionary stance of Paul in 1 Corinthians 9 and Acts" in L. E. Keck and J. L. Martyn (eds.), *Studies in Luke-Acts* (Nashville, TN: Abingdon, 1966), 203f. It seems to me that there is no real reason why the veracity of Luke should be doubted at this point, for the Jerusalem Council decision made it possible for a Jewish Christian such as Paul to endorse Jewish traditions— or at least some of them—without denying the principle of salvation by grace, as it was understood.

34. Bornkamm ("The missionary stance of Paul"), without any justification, doubts the accuracy of this episode as well.

35. Paul is using colorful language here to express generally the sacrifice which the converts were prepared to make, rather than indicating that he had had some physical ailment or other. See D. Guthrie, *Galatians* (Grand Rapids, MI: Eerdmans, 1981; London: Oliphants, 1974), 120.

36. See Sandmell, *Jewish Understanding of the New Testament*, 90.

37. J. Munch, *Paul and the Salvation of Mankind* (London: SCM Press, 1959), 204-5.

38. G. E. Ladd, *A Theology of the New Testament* (Grand Rapids, MI: Eerdmans, 1974; Guildford: Lutterworth).

39. Second century B.C.E.

40. Guthrie, *Galatians*.

41. Ibid., 117.

42. See, for example, *Intrepreter's Dictionary of the Bible*, vol. 3 (Nashville, TN: Abingdon, 1962).

43. Quoted by Joseph Grassi in *The Secret of Paul the Apostle* (Maryknoll: Orbis Books, 1978), 87.

44. See, e.g., S.G. Williamson, *Akan Religion and the Christian Faith* (Ghana Universities Press, 1965), 13f.

3. BIBLICAL AND OTHER INFLUENCES UPON MISSION

1. See my *Theology in Africa*, 97.

2. See my "The 'Methodist Society' — A Sect" in the *Ghana Bulletin of Theology* 2, 6; also *Aspects of Religion and Life in Africa* (Ghana Academy of Arts and Sciences, 1977).

3. See Margaret E. Thrall, ed., *First and Second Letters to the Corinthians* (Cambridge: Cambridge University Press, 1965), 3ff.

4. See my *Theology in Africa*, 166.

5. Quoted by Richard L. Rubenstein in "Religion and Cultural Synthesis" in *International Journal on the Unity of the Sciences* vol. 1, 1

(Spring 1988): 107. Rubenstein's article is a concise and illuminating discussion of the current of ideas underlying some aspects of Reformation thought.

6. A.C. McGiffert, *Protestant Thought Before Kant* (New York: Harper and Brothers, 1961), 1.

7. A.G. Dickens, *The English Reformation* (Cambridge, Mass.: Schocken, 1968; London: Collins, 1967), 92.

8. McGiffert, *Protestant Thought before Kant*, 25.

9. Dickens, *The English Reformation*, 94.

10. Rubenstein, "Religion and Cultural Synthesis," 111.

11. See Douglas S. Bax, "The Barmen Theological Declaration: Its Historical Background" in *Journal of Theology for Southern Africa* 47 (June 1984): 17.

12. Alasdair I. C. Heron, *A Century of Protestant Theology* (Philadelphia: Westminster John Knox, 1980; Guildford: Lutterworth, 1980), 79.

13. Ibid., 80.

14. See his *The Social Teachings of the Christian Churches*, vol. 2 (Chicago: University of Chicago Press, 1981), 470.

15. Ernst Troeltsch, *Christian Thought, Its History and Application* (Westport, Conn.: Hyperion, 1985; London: London University Press, 1923), 21-35.

16. See John Bright, *The Authority of the Old Testament* (Grand Rapids, Mich.: Baker, 1975; London: SCM Press, 1967), 63f.

17. See my *Theology in Africa*, 145f.

18. And also confessions, perhaps the most famous of them in this century being the Barmen Theological Declaration, issued in an attempt to stem Nazi excesses.

4. STRATEGY PRONOUNCEMENTS AND THEIR SIGNIFICANCE

1. A. Shorter, *African Christian Theology* (Maryknoll, NY: Orbis Books, 1975; London: Geoffrey Chapman, 1975), 150.

2. Quoted by Shorter, *African Christian Theology*, 20.

3. See my *Theology in Africa*, 11f.

4. *Ad Gentes*, 11. These and other quotations in this chapter are taken from Walter M. Abbott, S. J., and Very Rev. Msgr. Joseph Gallagher (eds.), *The Documents of Vatican II* (Piscataway, NJ: New Century, 1974; London: Geoffrey Chapman, 1966).

5. *Ad Gentes*, 25.

6. *L'Osservatore Romano* 9 (1028), February 29, 1988.

7. See my "The Minister—Then and Now" in J. S. Pobee (ed.),

Religion in a Pluralistic Society (Leiden: E. J. Brill, 1976), 172-73.

8. That is, in the as yet untapped mission fields.

9. *Ad Gentes*, 10.

10. *Collectanea Sacrae Congregationis de Propaganda Fide*, I (Rome: Typis Polyglottis Vaticanis, 1907), 42, n. 135.

11. See pp. 133-35 below.

12. *The Documents of Vatican II*, 662, n. 9.

13. See my "African Traditional Religion: Monotheism or Polytheism?" in I. J. Mowoe and R. Bjornson (eds.), *Africa and the West* (Westport, Conn.: Greenwood, 1986), 69-76.

14. Quoted by R. Pettazzoni, *Essays on the History of Religions* (Leiden: E. J. Brill, 1954), 1.

15. *Nostra Aetate*, 2.

16. Ibid.

17. *The Documents of Vatican II*, 662, n.11.

18. *Lumen Gentium*, 16.

19. See p. 97 above.

20. The Paulist Press edition, 25.

21. Pope John Paul II's address to Missionaries of the Sacred Hearts, *L'Osservatore Romano* 40 (1008), October 5, 1987, 16.

22. Vincent J. Donovan in Charles R. Taber (ed.), *The Church in Africa 1977* (So. Pasadena, Calif., William Carey Library, 1978), 105-6.

23. See p. 103 above.

24. See my *Theology in Africa*, 68-70.

25. Ibid., 177.

26. Charles Nyamiti, *The Way to Christian Theology in Africa* (Eldoret, Kenya: Gaba Publication [n.d.]), 55.

27. *Theology in Africa*, 109-11, 117.

28. Ibid.

29. C. R. Gaba, "Prayer in Anlo Religion."

30. See my "Christian and African Traditional Ceremonies" in *Practical Anthropology* 18, 2 (March-April 1971).

31. See especially his *Un visage africain du christianisme* (Paris, 1965).

32. Quoted in Shorter, *African Christian Theology*, 150.

33. Quoted ibid., 151-52.

34. John Mbiti, "Theological Impotence and the Universality of the Church" in G. H. Anderson and T. F. Stransky (eds.), *Mission Trends 3*, (Mahwah, N.J.: Paulist Press, 1976), 16.

35. See pp. 95-96 above, n. 6.

36. *L'Osservatore Romano* 46 (1014), November 16, 1987, 2.

37. *L'Osservatore Romano* 10 (1029), March 7, 1988, 3.

38. See the expression, "Once the elements of a particular culture

are seen truly to conform to the revealed message as held and transmitted by the Church. . . ."

39. Quite early in the course of the Western missionary effort in India there was a call for substituting the ancient Hindu scriptures for the Old Testament; see G. E. Phillips, *The Old Testament in the World Church* (Guildford: Lutterworth, 1942). For references here to the experimentation going on in India I am indebted to Dinesh D'Sousa's " 'Inculturation' — A Crisis in Indian Catholicism" in *The One World and I* (Washington: March 1988), 515f.

40. See p. 103 above.

41. H. Sawyerr, "Sin and Salvation: Soteriology Viewed from the African Situation" in Hans-Jurgen Becken (ed.), *Relevant Theology for Africa* (Durban: Lutheran Publishing House, 1973), 129ff.

42. Jack Goody, *Death, Property and the Ancestors* (Stanford, Calif.: Stanford University Press, 1962; London: Tavistock Publishers, 1962).

43. F. A. Arinze, *Sacrifice in Ibo Religion* (Ibadan: Ibadan University Press, 1970), 54.

44. Ibid., 83.

45. Gaba, "Prayer in Anlo Religion."

5. EXCLUSIVISM AND THE CHURCH TODAY

1. Donovan in Charles Taber (ed.), *The Church in Africa 1977*, 101.

2. See my *Aspects of Religion and Life in Africa* (Accra: Ghana Academy of Arts and Sciences, 1977), 19.

3. Ibid., 16f.

4. See Osofo-Okomfo Damuah's *Common Sense Series*, no. 8.

5. See Alfred G. Dunston, Jr., *The Black Man in the Old Testament and Its World* (Philadelphia: Dorance and Co., 1974), 26f.

6. Quoted from *Godianism*, a series of papers presented at the Conference of Traditional Religions of Nigeria, May 22, 1975, 2.

7. C. P. Groves, *The Planting of Christianity in Africa* IV (London: Lutterworth, 1958), 205-6.

8. Ibid., 205.

9. See the Constitution and Standing Orders of the Methodist Church, Ghana, no. 54 of which reads, "There shall be no drumming at a member's wake-keeping."

10. The Mennonites allow polygamists at the Lord's table.

11. The Methodist Church, Ghana, has taken steps to revise its Constitution, but it has yet to put an exposition of its faith into the hands of the ordinary member of the church.

12. E.g., G. C. Oosthuizen (ed.), *Religion Alive* (South Africa: Hodder and Stoughton, 1986), 197f.

13. Cited by Adrian Hastings, *A History of African Christianity 1950-1975* (Cambridge: Cambridge University Press, 1977), 225.

14. Norman E. Thomas, "The Future of the Church in Africa" in Charles Taber (ed.), *The Church in Africa 1977*, 197.

15. J. S. Mbiti, "The Biblical Basis for Present Trends in African Theology," in *Africa Theological Journal* 7, 2, 91.

16. B. G. M. Sundkler, *Bantu Prophets in South Africa* (Oxford: Oxford University Press, 1962), 277.

17. Ibid.

18. *The Road to Damascus: Kairos and Conversion* (Washington, D.C.: Center of Concern, 1989; London: CIIR, 1989).

19. Paul is not against women exercising charismatic gifts as such; what he seems to be upset about is the manner in which this is being done: the women are exercising these gifts without wearing a veil, which amounted to insubordination, since it is the man, "the image and glory of God," who is not to cover his head.

20. If Paul has the teaching ministry in mind here—and this is by no means certain—then he is falling back upon his Jewish background in which teaching was a male prerogative.

21. See pp. 43-48 above.

22. Itumeleng J. Mosala, "The Use of the Bible in Black Theology" in *Voices from the Third World* X, 2 (June 1987), 92.

23. Ibid.

24. I would add, "and every cultural area."

25. Fritz Stolz, *Interpreting the Old Testament* (London: SCM Press, 1975), 2.

26. Sundkler, *Bantu Prophets in South Africa* and my *Theology in Africa*.

27. See Theodor Gaster, *Myth, Legend, and Custom in the Old Testament* (New York: Harper and Row, 1975).

28. Saturday, March 19, 1983, No. 681.

29. See the promise to Abraham (Gen. 17) and the story of the Tower of Babel (Gen. 11).

30. Kwesi Dickson and Paul Ellingworth (eds.), *Biblical Revelation and African Beliefs* (Maryknoll, N.Y.: Orbis Books; Guildford: Lutterworth, 1969), 16.

31. In more than one Ghanaian language the God-name also means rain.

32. T. A. Beetham, *Christianity and the New Africa* (London: Pall Mall Press, 1967), 106-107.

33. See pp. 133-37.

6. CONCLUSION

1. See John Parratt (ed.), *A Reader in African Christian Theology* (London: SPCK, 1987).

2. Pp. 6-7.

Bibliography

JOURNALS

Bulletin of African Theology
International Review of Missions
Journal of Religion in Africa
Journal of Theology for Southern Africa
Missionalia
The Ecumenical Review
Voices from the Third World

BOOKS AND ARTICLES

Anderson, G. H. (ed.). *The Theology of the Christian Mission.* N.Y.: McGraw-Hill, 1961.

Anderson, G. H. and Stransky, T. F. (eds.). *Mission Trends 3.* Mahwah, N.J.: Paulist Press, 1976.

Appiah-Kubi, K. and Torres, S. (eds.). *African Theology en Route.* Maryknoll, N.Y.: Orbis Books, 1979.

Carters, C. W. and Earle, R. *The Acts of the Apostles.* Grand Rapids, Mich.: Zondervan Publishing House, 1973.

Dickens, A. G. *The English Reformation.* London: Collins, Fontana Library, 1967; New York: Schocken, 1968.

Dickson, K. A. *Aspects of Religion and Life in Africa.* Accra: Ghana Academy of Arts and Sciences, 1977.

———. *Theology in Africa.* Maryknoll, N.Y.: Orbis Books, 1984.

Flannery, Austin, O. P. (ed.). *Vatican II, the Conciliar and Post-Conciliar Documents*, 1981 edition. London: Fowler Wright Books, Ltd.; Collegeville, Minn.: Liturgical Press, 1983.

Hastings, Adrian. *A History of African Christianity 1950-1975.* Cambridge: Cambridge University Press, 1977.

Heron, Alasdair I. C. *A Century of Protestant Theology*. London: Lutterworth Press; Philadelphia: Westminster John Knox, 1980.

Johnson, L. T. *The Writings of the New Testament*. London: SCM Press; Minneapolis, Minn.: Augsburg Fortress, 1986.

Kaufmann, Yehezkel. *The Religion of Israel: From Its Beginnings to the Babylon Exile*. London: George Allen & Unwin, 1961; New York: Schocken, 1972.

Martyn, J. L. "A Law-Observant Mission to Gentiles: The Background to Galatians" in *Michigan Quarterly Review,* Vol. XXII, No. 3, Summer 1983.

Munch, J. *Paul and the Salvation of Mankind*. London: SCM Press, 1986.

Parratt, John (ed.). *A Reader in African Christian Theology*. London: SPCK, 1987.

Rubenstein, Richard L., "Religion and Cultural Synthesis," in *International Journal on the Unity of the Sciences*, Vol. 1, No. 1, Spring 1988.

Sanders, E. P. *Jesus and Judaism*. Philadelphia: Fortress Press, 1985.

Shorter, A. *African Christian Theology*. London: Geoffrey Chapman; Maryknoll, N. Y.: Orbis, 1975.

Taber, Charles R. (ed.). *The Church in Africa 1977*. Pasadena, Calif: William Carey Library, 1978.

Index

Acts of the Apostles, The
  and mission, 57-58
  and mission toward Gentiles,
    34-35, 38-40
  and Paul's speeches at Lystra
    and Athens, 42-43
  and role of Antioch in early
    church mission, 41-42
Adaptation (adaptionism), 93-95,
  105
  in Africa, 96
  and Catholic church, 112
  opposition to, 111
Ad Gentes, 95, 97
African church
  and biblical interpretation,
    132-42
  and exclusivism, 132-33, 137
  independent, 129-32
African religion
  and African life, 142-45
  and Christian teaching of sal-
    vation, 122
  and sacrifices, 121-22
African theology, 158
African traditions
  incorporation into church of,
    106-10
  libation, 106-7
  music, 108

  naming ceremony, 108
  prayer, 108
Afrikania Mission, 126-27
Antioch, role of in Gentile outreach, 41-42
Bible translations, 139-40
Biblical interpretation
  and African church, 131-42,
    154-55
  and Christ's death, 147
  and cultural context, 145-46,
    153
  and exclusivism, 132-33, 137,
    154
  and human dignity, 147
  macro level of, 153-54
  micro level of, 154
Catholic policy
  and church traditions, 119
  on other religions, 100-106,
    113-16
  on pluralism, 111-12
Christian distinctiveness, 116-19
Christianity and African religion
  and culture, 125-26, 157-58
Circumcision, Pauline view of,
  52-53
Council of Jerusalem, 45-47, 53
Creeds, 86-87, 89-90
Early church, the
  and continuity between Juda-

ism and Christianity, 37
and influence of Old Testament, 29
role of Antioch in, 41-42
Education, 2-3
Egypt, influence on Israel's religion, 9-10
Evangelii Praecones, 103
Exclusivism, 3-6
in Africa, 85-86, 129, 132
and biblical interpretation, 132-33, 137, 154
and Catholic policy, 123
in the church, 104
and creeds, 86
historical, 85
Galatians, Letter to the, 48-51, 54-55
and Judaisers, 56-57
and mission, 57-58
and pagan religions, 56, 57
Gentiles
early church's attitude toward, 39-40
Jesus' attitude toward, 32-34
Jewish attitude toward, 32
and Pauline churches, 51
Hellenistic Jews, 35-37
Incarnation, 111
Inculturation, 114-16
Israel, ancient
and Canaan, 10-11, 18-19, 66
Egypt's influence on, 9-10
exiles of, 13
and other nations' gods, 11-12
postexilic period of, 13-15
proselytism of, 26-27
punishment of with non-Israelite peoples, 17-18
relationship of with non-Jews, 25-26
and Samaritans, 13-14

view of her religion, 8-9
Jesus Christ
attitude toward Gentiles, 32-34
attitude toward Judaism, 30-32, 34
Libation (African ritual of), 106-7
Lumen Gentium, 102-3
Malachi (book of), 21-24
Methodist Society, the, 73
Mission
and adaptation, 93-95
in *Ad Gentes*, 95, 97
and Barth, 82-83
as "civilizing" process, 124
and Harnack, 83-84
in *Lumen Gentium*, 102-3
modern exclusivist attitude of, 62-63, 65
and the New Testament, 67-76
in *Nostra Aetate*, 99, 102
and Old Testament attitudes, 61-67
and the Reformation, 76, 81-82
rules and regulations' effect on, 73-76
and Schleiermacher, 83-84
and Troeltsch, 83
as Westernization, 125-26
New Testament
and Gospel view of Gentiles, 32-33
and mission, 67-76
Nostra Aetate, 99, 102
Old Testament
evidence for God's involvement with other traditions, 15-18, 19
Harnack's view of, 84
inclusion of non-Jews, 25-26
as influenced by non-Israelite

ideas and practices, 20-21
influence on early church, 29
and Israel's view of her relig-
    ion, 8-9
and mission, 61-67
perception of other nations'
    gods, 11-12
Schleiermacher's views of, 84
Paul, the Apostle
    and circumcision, 52-53
    and Council of Jerusalem, 46
    and Jewish traditions, 47-48
    and relationship with other
        apostles, 50-51
    and relationship with pagan
        world, 71
    view of pagan religions, 42-43,
        56, 68
Pluralism, 111-12
Proselytism, 26-27
Redemptoris Missio, 105
Reformation, the
    background to, 77-81

and Luther's view of Scrip-
    tures, 80-81
and missions, 76, 81-82
Salvation, 120-22
Scriptures
    African approach to, 148-53
    and macro level of under-
        standing, 153-54
    and micro level of understand-
        ing, 154
Stephen
    and continuity between Juda-
        ism and Christianity, 38
    and Hellenistic Jews, 37
    and Jewish traditions, 37-38
Tabula rasa, 124
Vatican II, 93, 95
    and African religion, 98-99
    and view of other religions,
        100-106
Vital union, 109
Westernism (Westernization),
    125-26, 128-29, 130, 151

Also of Interest

TRANSFORMING MISSION
Paradigm Shifts in Theology of Mission
by David Bosch
Covers the entire sweep of Christian mission, attending to the interplay of the *theological* and the *historical* as paradigms for the understanding and praxis of Christian mission. Overcoming modern skepticism and achieving a position that holds competing truths in dialectical tension, Bosch helps us integrate the passion of Jesus's mission and the church's contemporary way of the cross.

"Well-informed and courageous. . . ." — Hans Küng

650pp. ISBN 0-88344-719-3 Paperback
     ISBN 0-88344-744-4 Clothbound

TRANSLATING THE MESSAGE
Missionary Impact on Culture
by Lamin Sanneh
Explores the often-surprising consequences of missionary activity— especially translation—on cultures, from the early days of Christianity to the twentieth century.

"An exciting new story of Christian mission." — *The Christian Century*

310pp. ISBN 0-88344-361-9 Paperback

HEARING AND KNOWING
Theological Reflections on Christianity in Africa
by Mercy Amba Oduyoye
Reflects on early Christianity in Africa, the impact of missionaries from the First World, the contextualization of theology, feminism, and traditional doctrines.

"Outstanding and completely refreshing." — *Mission Focus*

176pp. ISBN 0-88344-258-2 Paperback

MY FAITH AS AN AFRICAN
by Jean-Marc Éla
In a bold call to action, the Cameroonian theologian challenges us to reread the Gospels through African eyes.

"Exciting and moving. . . . His is the strongest theological voice in sub-Saharan Africa." — Marie Giblin

176pp. ISBN 0-88344-631-6 Paperback

WEST AFRICAN CHRISTIANITY
The Religious Impact
by Lamin Sanneh
Explores the thesis that the African — as agent of religious adaptation — has played a more critical role in Christian development than the missionary counterpart.

"A fresh new map with a new perspective." — *Missiology*

286pp. ISBN 0-88344-703-7 Paperback

AFRICAN CRY
by Jean-Marc Ela
To become truly African, Ela argues, the church must reject colonial structures imposing Western symbols and culture, reject a view of God as uninterested in the socio-political realities of Africa, and accept the liberating God of the Exodus.

"Especially welcome. . . ." — *The Tablet*

160pp. ISBN 0-88344-259-0 Paperback